To Be a Worker

A book in the series

**Latin America in Translation /
en Traducción / em Tradução**

Sponsored by the
Duke–University of North Carolina
Joint Program in Latin American Studies

TO BE A
WORKER

IDENTITY AND
POLITICS IN
PERU

Jorge Parodi

Translated by
James Alstrum
Catherine Conaghan

Edited, with an Introduction, by
Catherine Conaghan

The University of North Carolina Press
Chapel Hill and London

331.767
P25t

Originally published in Spanish as
"Ser obrero es algo relativo . . .": Obreros, Clasimo y Política
(Lima: Instituto de Estudios Peruanos, 1986), © IEP ediciones.

Manufactured in the United States of America

The paper in this book meets the guidelines for permanence and
durability of the Committee on Production Guidelines for Book
Longevity of the Council on Library Resources.

Library of Congress Cataloging-in-Publication Data
Parodi Solari, Jorge.
[Ser obrero es algo relativo—English]
To be a worker : identity and politics in Peru / by Jorge Parodi ;
translated by James Alstrum and Catherine Conaghan ;
edited, with an introduction, by Catherine Conaghan.
p. cm.—(Latin America in translation/en traducción/em tradução)
Includes index.
ISBN 0-8078-2548-4 (cloth : alk. paper)
ISBN 0-8078-4860-3 (pbk. : alk. paper)
1. Metal-workers—Peru. 2. Working class—Peru.
3. Trade-unions—Peru. I. Conaghan, Catherine. II. Title. III. Series.

HD8039.M52 P4613 2000
331.7′671′0985—dc21

99-049579

04 03 02 01 00   5 4 3 2 1

To Angel and Judith

Contents

Glossary of Spanish Terms ix

Introduction to the English Translation by
Catherine Conaghan xi

Part I. A History about Workers, a Union, and Politics

Introduction 3

1. Becoming a Factory Worker 10

2. Standing Up for Yourself as a Worker 23

3. Fighting for Benefits: The Limits of the Clasista Union 38

4. Acting Like Workers 57

5. To Be a Worker Is Relative: Industry and the Limits
to (Re)Producing Workers 72

6. Amid Frustration, Indignation, and Fear 85

Part II. In His Own Words: The Many Lives of Jesús Zúñiga

7. Childhood: We'd Be Winners Someday 99

8. Lima: The Light Seemed Like Daylight 102

9. Everything Was Great When I Started at
the Factory 104

10. Hard Workers and Shirkers 107

11. The Union: We Were No Longer What We
Were Before 109

12. Deceived by the Company, but Hopeful
in the Struggle 112

13. Jesús and Politics 114

14. If This Turns Out OK, to Hell with the Company 119

15. Breaking Bread 121

CONTENTS

16. Retirement: Political Disillusion, New Horizons 123

17. The Unión Grauina: The President Is Also a Peruvian 125

18. Defending the Absent 132

Part III. Conclusion

19. Unstable Processes, Radical Actions, Precarious Relationships, and Relative Identities 135

20. What Can You Hope For?: Jesús in the 1990s 144

Epilogue 151

Appendix: Selected Political Chronology of Peru, 1968–1995 159

Notes 163

Index 171

Glossary of Spanish Terms

argolla: ring; refers to the system of clientelism organized in the factory based on the regional background of workers. The system was used by bosses to control the labor force.

apurimeño(s): person(s) from the department of Apurímac.

caudillo/caudillismo: strongman, boss, bossism; used in the text to refer to union leaders.

chalaco(s): person(s) from the port city of Callao.

cholo(s): person(s) of indigenous background who migrate(s) to the city; the term is frequently used in Peru in a derogatory manner to indicate that someone is nonwhite, lower class, and poorly educated.

clasista/clasismo: refers to the militant class-centric ideology adopted by parties of the Left and the trade union movement in Peru.

compañero(s): comrade, friend, co-worker; a form of address frequently used by people on the political Left; also a form of address frequently employed among members of the APRA Party in Peru.

criollo(s): person(s) from coastal Peru, especially applied to persons from Lima; the term also may connote that someone is prone to trickery.

foco: nucleus; term used in Che Guevara's philosophy of guerrilla warfare.

Fujimorismo: refers to the political ideas and practices of President Alberto Fujimori.

grauino(s): person(s) from the province of Grau in the department of Apurímac.

la lucha: the struggle; refers to the militant strategy of protests, work stoppages, and strikes advocated by the New Left and clasista trade unions.

la nueva izquierda: the New Left; refers to a range of new leftist political organizations that appeared in Peru in the 1970s. Vanguardia Revolucionaria was among the parties that appeared in this wave.

limeño(s): person(s) from the capital city of Lima.

pueblos jovenes: young towns; the term was coined during the Velasco government to refer to the squatter settlements around the city of Lima.

sectores populares: popular sectors; lower and lower middle classes.

serrano(s): person(s) from the interior highlands of Peru, the sierra.

sierra: interior highlands of Peru.

sol(es): unit(s) of Peru's currency.

talareño(s): person(s) from the northern province of Talara in the department of Piura.

Introduction to the English Translation

This book is a worker's story. It is also the story of what happened to a working class and a nation's politics.

Like thousands of Peruvians in the 1960s and 1970s, Jesús Zúñiga made his way from the provinces to the capital city of Lima. He eventually found work in a metallurgical factory on Avenida Argentina in the city's industrial zone. The long journey that brought Jesús to the gates of Metal Empresa began when he left his peasant family in the *sierra*. Migration meant the start of a life of labor marked by uncertainty and constant change. In transit from childhood to manhood, Jesús worked as a busboy, a street vendor, and a construction worker before he landed a factory job. For the masses of migrants streaming out of the countryside to Lima, the city stood as the gateway to social and economic mobility.[1] To Jesús, the bright lights of Lima "seemed like daylight," and the prospect of a better life seemed real.

In a volatile labor market, landing a steady job was an important leap forward for young men like Jesús looking to get ahead. But Jesús' struggle for a better life did not end once he secured a job at Metal Empresa. In fact, it was just the beginning. Like other industrial workers, the employees of Metal Empresa found themselves in a constant struggle to make ends meet, to win respect and decent treatment in the workplace, and ultimately to liberate themselves from the confines of factory life.

As a young sociologist, Jorge Parodi chronicled the multiple struggles and the complicated lives of the workers of Metal Empresa. Like most social scientists of his generation, Parodi was schooled in Marxist theory, and his leftist sympathies drew him to study the social actors that had been identified by Peru's Left as agents of revolutionary change. As Parodi learned, workers were changing the face of Peru's society and politics, though not always in the ways originally envisioned by strategists on the Left. In the 1970s, militant workers and leftist movements shared center stage with the military government of General Juan Velasco Alvarado that declared itself to be "nationalist and revolutionary." But the radical politics of the 1970s was not a prelude to social revolution. The military experiment failed. Working-class identity and working-class attachment to the Left were already in question by the 1980s. The breakdown in the relationship between workers and the Left eventually opened the door to the technocratic "antipolitics" espoused by the political newcomer of 1990, Alberto Fujimori.

Through the narratives of Jesús and the workers of Metal Empresa, Parodi tracks the making and unmaking of Peru's industrial working class. In doing so, he helps us understand how workers grappled with the transformations taking place in their own lives and the world around them. In the stark monologues of Jesús and his *compañeros,* we come to appreciate the significance of what workers won in their struggles. We also come to know something of what was lost as the economic crisis of the 1980s bore down on workers and forced them into an even more desperate scramble to keep their families fed.

It has become part of the current orthodoxy in Peru to demonize the military government of General Juan Velasco Alvarado (1968–75).[2] Yet Parodi's account forcefully reminds us of the cruel treatment that reigned in workplaces before the new regime of labor laws introduced by Velasco. As the workers of Metal Empresa tell it, physical exploitation and psychological abuse were part of the daily fare in the nonunionized factory. Workers toiled without breaks, were forced to buy their own supplies, and wolfed down their lunches while standing on street corners "as if they were nobodies." Complaints about working conditions were resolved by firing those who dared to speak up. The carrot and the stick were used to maintain discipline on the shop floor. Bosses cultivated clientelism, creating a privileged group of workers in the plant who, in turn, policed the behavior of other workers. At the same time, cultural differences between the hometown *limeños* and the migrant *serranos* bred rivalries and mistrust that kept workers apart and divided in the ways they attempted to cope with factory life.

The wretched conditions came to an end in 1970 with the promulgation of two laws by the Velasco government: the Ley de Estabilidad Laboral (Law of Security of Employment) and the decree that created the Comunidad Industrial (Industrial Community). The laws were a frontal assault on the skewed power relations in plants and set the stage for an explosive growth of trade unionism. The Industrial Community reform stipulated that a formal institutional body (Comunidad Industrial) be created in industrial firms to oversee workers' participation in profits and shareholding in firms. The Security of Employment Law obligated firms to tenure workers after a three-month trial period, making it very difficult to fire workers thereafter.[3]

The reaction to this unprecedented legal breakthrough in workers' rights can only be described as euphoric. In Metal Empresa, workers celebrated and cried at hearing the news of Establidad Laboral. There is perhaps no more poignant evidence of workers' desperate desire to attain job security than their willingness to sustain injury by staging on-the-job accidents. One worker confessed to Parodi that he had burned his own hand with a blowtorch to ensure that his name would be kept on the company's roster long enough to pass the probationary period to obtain job security. It was a terrible trade-off that many workers were willing to make to assure themselves a stable income in an otherwise unpredictable labor market.

Without the threat of dismissal hanging over their heads, workers were quick to unionize. The Velasco government presided over the most rapid expansion in unionization in the history of Peru.[4] As the workers of Metal Empresa tell it, unionization changed everything. Most important, it established the ability of workers to claim their rights, to be treated "like dignified workers" instead of "nobodies." Getting a company cafeteria, instead of being forced to eat standing on the street corner, was just one of the many gains that workers enjoyed as a result of unionization. The union was not only a vehicle that delivered material goods to workers, it was the line of defense against all the despotic practices that had previously prevailed on the shop floor. Union leaders aggressively defended their members in disputes with management. The old clientelistic practices that workers had used to ensure themselves tolerable treatment, from bringing the boss a chicken to taking him out to the local bordello, were no longer needed. Protection was now assured by the raised voices and the audacious actions of young, strident union leaders.

The remarkable militancy of the Peruvian labor movement in the 1970s was fueled by the confluence of ideas and attitudes known as *clasismo*.[5] Clasismo identified class struggle as the strategy through which industrial workers and popular classes could secure their long-denied rights and reclaim their dignity in Peruvian society. That struggle, *la lucha,* was manifested in persistent mobilization. Protests, demonstrations, marches, work actions, and strikes were the currency of clasismo. Negotiation or collaboration with the establishment—employers or state officials—was viewed negatively by *clasistas*. Defending the autonomy of class organizations from the state was a central component of clasista thinking. Indeed, the decision by the Communist Party–controlled Confederación General de Trabajadores del Perú (CGTP) to lend its "critical support" to the Velasco government alienated many workers and unions associated with the clasista line. The CGTP later abandoned its support of the military regime when Velasco was replaced by General Francisco Morales Bermúdez. Labor resistance to the antireform, fiscally conservative policies of Morales Bermúdez was expressed in two massive general strikes in July 1977 and May 1978. After the 1977 strike, the government announced a plan for a transition back to civilian rule.[6]

In Metal Empresa, unionization went hand in hand with the diffusion of clasista ideology. As Parodi underscores, the nexus that developed between young leftist activists and workers was crucial for the development of the union and its leadership.[7] Radical university students helped workers with the legal procedures involved in creating a union and provided logistical help in strikes. In turn, workers were recruited into the ranks of left-wing politics. As the quid pro quo for the support they received, union leaders and activists were expected to be active members in the party cell and effective political bosses in the factory.

The activation of trade unionism, the political awakening of the popular classes, and hastening the end of the military dictatorship were unmistakable achievements spearheaded by the Peruvian Left. But almost as soon as these accomplishments were realized, the Left began to lose its grip on the workers that it had labored so hard to win over. Parodi's analysis vividly elucidates the tensions that led to a political estrangement of historic consequence.

Stuck in its own rhetoric asserting the revolutionary character of the proletariat, the Peruvian Left failed to appreciate fully the complexity of workers' lives and the fluid nature of their identity. As poor people trained in the arts of survival, workers simultaneously pursued multiple economic strategies designed to keep their households afloat. Their identity as workers was always relative, always tempered by dreams of escaping the proletarian life.[8] As Jesús tells us, even as a child he had hoped to become a "businessman." Jesús was a dedicated union leader, but he also never stopped trying out new business schemes in the precious little spare time he had. One of the most memorable moments of Jesús' oral history is his tale of a failed poultry business. "To hell with the company!" exclaims one of Jesús' partners as he savors the idea of future economic success and an imminent departure from the factory. Unfortunately, the fledgling business folded and Jesús' unending quest to secure a decent income continued.

For workers, participation in the union was but one of many strategies to improve the quality of their lives. The pragmatism of workers and their desire for immediate economic gains did not always jibe with the broader goals of the union or dispose workers to endless political mobilization. Workers resented the constant demands that union leaders made for their presence at political protests. Nor did their economic calculations always coincide with the principles of solidarity and equity defended by union leaders. In flat defiance of union directives, workers accepted company deals in certain matters which violated the terms of their collective contract. The onset of a severe economic recession in 1983 sapped workers of the will to put their paychecks at risk by involving themselves in strikes and work stoppages. Each successive retreat undermined and demoralized union leaders. Rather than rallying workers to defend their jobs, union leaders found themselves in the strange circumstances of negotiating on severance pay packages that facilitated the downsizing of industries and progressively weakened trade unionism.

The strain in the relations between union leaders and the rank and file was one of the factors driving a wedge between the Left and its working-class base. Partisan in-fighting among leftist groups and their neglect of continuing grassroots work was another. The Left's endless internal bickering over ideological positions and leadership struggles confused and alienated workers. Moreover, the end of the military dictatorship and the return to civilian rule in 1980 dramatically altered the Left's relationship to the political system. Leftist parties and movements were no longer outsiders and street fighters, they were entities with electoral ambitions and power brokers inside the system. In the first half of the 1980s, Izquierda Unida, a loose electoral coalition of Left parties, turned into the second largest vote winner in the country. Leftist leaders who had previously been in constant contact with trade unions now turned their attention to congress and municipal governments. Facing businesses that reneged on collective contracts, an ambivalent rank and file, and a distant political class, trade union militants felt increasingly isolated.[9]

For both union leaders and workers, the options were exit or rage. Jesús resigned as union leader and left the factory to set up his own metalworking shop. Remaining union leaders expressed their fury with what they viewed as the company's duplicitous business practices by staging plant occupations on three occasions between 1980 and 1984. During one of the takeovers, excited protesters made it a point to call Jorge Parodi so that he would have the opportunity to witness clasismo in action.

For workers who stayed behind in the industries ravaged by the economic recession, plummeting wages took their toll on every aspect of life. Eugenio Vilcapoma vividly described the downward spiral of his life in the period 1980–84 when he had to support a family solely on his wages from Metal Empresa. He talked about the effects of declining purchasing power in a way that no economist could. Reflecting on the protein-deficient diet forced on his family by poverty, Eugenio strained to remember the taste of milk and sadly noted the progressive disappearance of meat and fish from his family's dinner table. He spoke of the loss of sociability and reciprocity. No longer could family and friends afford the celebrations and gift-giving of the past. "I've been really having a horrible life," concluded Eugenio.

That "horrible life," concluded Parodi, was not forging a revolutionary class. As he looked out on the panorama of working life in the 1980s, Parodi saw people engaged in a fierce struggle to assure the survival of their urban households. Patching together a variety of income-generating activities was the key to survival; no single occupation (or identity or political strategy) sufficed.

The first edition of Parodi's study was published in October 1986 as "*Ser obrero es algo relativo . . .*" (To be a worker is something relative). Among left intellectuals, the book received a cool reception. Its conclusions flew in the face of the orthodox view of the working class as a revolutionary agent.[10] Moreover, at the time of its publication, the notion of a political and economic eclipse of the working class appeared to be wrong to many activists and analysts. In 1986, Peru was still in the honeymoon phase of the presidency of Alan García (1985–90). His populist economic policies and his progressive rhetoric won him substantial support from the Left and labor. With García pumping up the economy, industrial production underwent some recovery and García's active courting of the domestic business elite appeared to be laying the groundwork for the rejuvenation of the industrial sector. If anything, the conditions in the first half of the García government favored a revival of the industrial working class as an economic and political protagonist. Analysts reading "*Ser obrero*" in 1986 believed that Parodi's findings had been distorted because his fieldwork had taken place during the short-term economic recession of 1983–84 and were based on one case study in one of the industrial branches most severely hit by the recession.

By the 1990s, however, Parodi's analysis did not seem wrong. On the contrary, it seemed prescient. The Left's optimism about labor's revival and the potential for social and economic transformation had given way to shock and disbelief as Peru stood at the brink of total disaster. Under the second half of the García presidency, economic decline and guerrilla warfare converged to produce the worst crisis in Peru's contemporary history.[11] García's economic policies, which combined increased public spending, an expansion in the money supply, and a general framework of price controls, ended in severe hyperinflation. In 1989, the inflation rate for the year was close to 3,000 percent; by 1990, the yearly rate stood at a mind-boggling 7,650 percent. Workers were especially hard hit as hyperinflation shrunk paychecks.[12]

As the economy collapsed, growing political violence added to the widespread sensation that Peru was heading toward a catastrophe. Despite the military's pursuit through the 1980s, the Maoist guerrilla movement Sendero Luminoso had continued to grow along with another Marxist group, Movimiento Revolucionario Tupac Amaru.[13] Starting in 1988, Sendero embarked on a new strategy to establish its presence in Lima. The strategy included acts of terrorism such as car bombings with a campaign aimed at infiltrating and taking over popular class organizations in the poor shantytown neighborhoods surrounding Lima. By the early 1990s, the death toll from a decade of war stood at over thirteen thousand persons.

The already diminishing electoral appeal of the legal Left was undermined further by an official split of the Izquierda Unida into two competing factions for the 1990 presidential election. Alienated from the traditional parties, low-income voters in Lima's shantytowns and inner city neighborhoods looked for another alternative. They found it in the unconventional presidential candidacy of a political newcomer, Alberto Fujimori, and his Cambio 90 movement.

Fujimori's electoral strategy did not focus on the fast-fading industrial proletariat. Rather, he focused on the working masses—all those people just like Jesús whose households crisscrossed the formal and informal sectors of the economy. He spoke directly to the concerns of these voters and their dreams of building their own small businesses. He projected the image of a no-nonsense, hardworking person who would focus on prag-matic solutions to the day-to-day problems of working people. His pledge to promote "honesty, technology, and work" was an appealing antidote to the grandiose, unfulfilled promises made by the parties in the past.[14]

The appeal paid off. Fujimori won strong support in election districts with working-class and informal sector voters. Fujimori's near 25 percent of the national vote in the first round of the 1990 election was double the Left's 11 percent of the vote that was divided among its two competing candidates. Fujimori easily defeated his center-right rival, Mario Vargas Llosa, in the second round of the presidential election by polling 56.5 per-cent of the vote.

Low-income working people were the core constituency behind Fuji-mori's electoral victory in 1990 and his subsequent reelection in 1995. This constituency was supportive of the measures that Fujimori took to "re-store order" in the chaotic environment. The austerity measures taken by the government were painful but found popular acceptance because they put an end to hyperinflation. Fujimori's *auto-golpe* of April 1992, which shut down congress and suspended the 1979 constitution, won majoritarian approval across all social sectors, including the lowest income groups.[15] After the coup, Fujimori presided over the writing of a new constitution that overturned the long-standing legal ban on immediate presidential re-election.

In the period leading up to the 1995 election, Fujimori sought to con-nect with low-income voters once again through public works spending on schools, clinics, parks, and roads in the urban shantytowns and in rural areas. In an overwhelming victory, Fujimori won 64 percent of the vote and an absolute majority in congress. The once powerful electoral force of the Left, Izquierda Unida, polled less than 1 percent of the vote in the presidential race and less than 2 percent in the congressional election.

Utilitarian considerations were the driving force in the relationship be-tween the working masses and President Fujimori. The president's ca-pacity to "deliver the goods" was the source of his popularity in the period from 1990 through 1995. The elimination of the threats to physical security posed by terrorism, the restoration of a stable macroeconomic order, and the provision of basic infrastructure were policy achievements that made a meaningful difference in the everyday lives of people.[16]

Fujimorismo, however, was never a project that aspired to organize and empower working people in any significant way. Fujimori's movement,

Cambio 90–Nueva Mayoría was never more than a sobriquet used to group together his handpicked congressional deputies. Through the social assistance programs run by the Ministerio de la Presidencia, the government sought to undercut the autonomy of grassroots organizations and municipalities. Moreover, as Parodi reminds us in his epilogue, trade unionism was dealt a definitive blow in the course of the neoliberal economic restructuring undertaken by the Fujimori administration. What remained of the hard-won rights established in the 1970s were stripped away. Job security, the right to strike, and the legal standing of collective contracts all fell by the wayside in the neoliberal reforms of labor law. Employers took advantage of the deregulation to hire more temporary workers or to subcontract jobs to employment agencies. These practices further weakened the hold of trade unions.

Fujimorismo took advantage of the anomic and atomized state of Peruvian society. The demobilizing calculus of Fujimorismo in the 1990s was the antithesis of what the Left in the 1970s had championed in the ideology of clasismo. The Left's insistence on combative participation and mass mobilization was replaced by Fujimori's call for pragmatism and his view of politics as an exercise in efficient management by technocrats. While the Left had exhorted workers to be agents of political and social transformation, Fujimori emphasized the benefits of a retreat from politics and an embrace of the forces of the market.

In the years immediately following the publication of this book, Jorge Parodi continued to write about the perspectives and the problems of popular classes in Peru.[17] He eventually left sociology for a career as a psychoanalyst. Jesús struggled to keep his metal repair shop going on Avenida Argentina. Metal Empresa went bankrupt in 1988, leaving its workers to fend for themselves.

Jorge Parodi, Jesús Zúñiga, and the workers of Metal Empresa have gone their separate ways, but they left us with an invaluable document for understanding how Peru's recent past continues to shape its politics. While some readers may find the end of this book disheartening, its principal arguments do leave room for optimism. Working people in Peru are pragmatic—but this does not mean that their alignment with the "antipolitics" embodied in Fujimorismo is permanent or that their struggle for dignity and fairness has ceased. As this book shows, structural conditions in the economy profoundly shape the consciousness and political behavior of working people, but so do leaders and organizations.

The reduction in the size of the traditional, industrial working class and the weakening of trade unionism have not diminished the centrality of working people to national politics, but they have been flung out into a world of work in constant flux and identities formed around jobs are not fixed. Progressive politics is not dead, but its protagonists and its staging grounds are more diverse than ever. The substantial scholarly literature on social movements in Latin America points to the numerous venues (neighborhoods, churches, soup kitchens) and identities (defined by gender, region, ethnicity) that form the bases of important popular struggles.[18] Indeed, it is the enormous diversity of social movements in Peru and the rest of Latin America that poses the greatest challenge for political activists seeking to turn these forces into organizations that can shape national politics in a sustained way.

Even after he left the union and factory life, Jesús continued to be active in community organizing. He concluded his conversation with Jorge Parodi in a commentary on leadership. He advised all would-be leaders of workers to be "loyal" and remain close to those they seek to represent. Maybe a new generation of leaders will heed that advice and build organizations that advance the interests of working people in ways that respect their aspirations and their right to define their own future. There still may be reason to hope that Peruvian workers might one day realize the possibilities that Jesús once felt as he looked out on Lima's lights.

—Catherine Conaghan

PART I

A History about Workers, a Union, and Politics

Introduction

They are indispensable but uneasy partners of business and industry. They cause political troubles for every government. They have been at the forefront of monumental social struggles. Some people think of them as "manual labor." In the view of others, they are the principal agents of the social transformation that Peru needs. Nevertheless, despite their importance in economic, social, and political life, industrial workers are not as familiar to us as they should be. Perhaps that is because they are rarely given the chance to tell us about themselves.

What does it really mean today to be an industrial worker in Lima? How is their typical organization, the union, set up? What effects does unionization have on relationships between workers and employers? Why do workers choose to press their demands by striking? What were the relationships that arose between workers and leftist parties in the realm of political and union activity? Simply put, I wondered about workers and wage relations, the origins of their social identity and unionism, and the role they play in my country's politics.

The original inspiration for this research came in a conversation with Angel Gallardo, a well-known former labor leader of the sheet metal workers. He observed: "The great majority of workers have a capitalist mentality: put your money together, get your severance pay, and set up a business which is usually as a street peddler or hawker." His insight was so compelling that I decided to explore the peculiarities of Peruvian industrial workers further. No matter how you look at it, Gallardo's observation suggested that the identity and aspirations of workers were far more relative than standard, static concepts such as "proletariat" and "working class" implied. And these were concepts that were used frequently in social and political analysis in Peru from the 1960s through the 1980s.

I subsequently interviewed other union leaders who confirmed Gallardo's observation but also qualified it. Walter Huatuco, a worker in Candados Peruanos for thirteen years and a leader of the Federación Metalúrgica, argued that the desire for economic independence did not preclude the search for job security on the part of industrial workers. The factory worker actually "evaluates the company's situation a lot: if it's good, if it's going to be secure, if you can retire from it. The identity of being a worker goes along with job security but at the same time he thinks: I'll work for five years; I'll save five million soles [Peruvian currency] and then I'll work outside on the street. To be a worker is relative." Indeed, according to Jorge Villón, a union leader from Metal Empresa, this wish to be on your own and self-employed appears as soon as job security is achieved: "You enter the factory with the idea of having a job, with the aim of securing stable employment. You get in on the ground floor and you go on learning. But when you get job security, you begin to change your outlook and wish for more. Once you get to become a permanent, full-time worker, you look for a way to get out of it."

Javier Donayre, a leader of the Federación de Trabajadores de la Industria de Papeles, made me realize that the dreams of workers in nonmetallurgical industries were the same. According to Donayre, the relatively high wages in a paper-producing company like Papelera Atlas allowed workers "to amass capital and have other businesses of their own, a taxi or a small farm. Some think that this is better than the factory and they quit at any time."

I conducted my field research with workers in a company named Metal Empresa. My first discovery was that these workers had shown a surprising unwillingness to fight for their jobs when the company threatened to cut back personnel in 1977. The company offered a severance package to any worker who wanted to quit. Out of a total workforce of 420 persons, 120 workers took advantage of the offer as a way to amass enough capital to underwrite a small independent business. In the face of the workers' willingness to quit, the union did not even propose a strategy opposing cutbacks. The union had been a militant organization that espoused clasismo, an ideology prevalent in Peru during this period. Clasismo was a worldview that emphasized the importance of social class and the class struggle. It dominated the thinking and strategies of the Peruvian Left in the 1960s and 1970s. Nonetheless, this formerly militant, clasista union found itself thrust into the position of negotiating with the company about the amount of severance pay in the benefits package rather than undertaking a full-fledged defense of its workers.

In any case, I found that many workers who were not affected by the personnel cutbacks left to open up their own small businesses. Between

1976 and 1978, a group made up of the most well-known clasista leaders of the union established a small workshop to make metal products. One of them, Celestino Peralta, would later become a legend for prospering in the bakery business. Finally, among the workers who stayed on in the factory, there was one group that ran their own businesses concurrently: grocery stores in their homes, metallurgical workshops or services, and other small enterprises.

This situation puzzled me. How do you explain the unwillingness of workers to fight for their jobs, the readiness to negotiate with an employer about leaving the company, the desire (even among recognized clasista union leaders) to give up their positions as wage earners or juggle wage-earning and entrepreneurial activities? All this was going on among workers who were relatively well paid and unionized. They were workers who were singled out by the government as being among the "privileged" in society. The political Left called them the vanguard class, the proletariat, perfect revolutionaries.

National accounts statistics show the importance of industry as a producer and employer in Peru's economy. In 1982, industry accounted for 23.4 percent of the gross domestic product, and employed 12.6 percent of the economically active population. Because of the exploratory nature of my study and my desire to investigate various dimensions of the world of industrial workers (also in part because of limits on resources), I chose to do a case study. I chose Metal Empresa, a company with 247 employees in 1984 (184 factory workers and 63 office workers), because it was among the firms with more than 200 employees. Firms of this size employed 45 percent of the wage earners in the manufacturing industry in the early 1980s.[1] In short, Metal Empresa was representative of companies that provided an important portion of the jobs in the industrial sector. It was a metallurgical company devoted to producing metal ships (its main line of products in the 1970s), diverse metal structures, boilers for industry, and other metal products. In industrial terminology, it was a branch of the metal products manufacturing business. At the time, it was a very important branch of industry in Peru. In 1983, metal products accounted for 13 percent of the gross value of manufacturing production and took third place behind food processing and the chemical industry.

For the purpose of studying unions, the case of Metal Empresa was ideal. The union was founded in 1970, and it became famous among the workers' unions on Avenida Argentina for its combativeness and the wide

range of benefits it won. Its prestige was even greater among the metallurgical unions because of the outstanding participation of two of its leaders
in the Federación Metalúrgica and its constant participation in demonstrations and work stoppages called by the Federación. In other words, the
case study allowed me to analyze the way in which the transition toward a
workers' organization came about and the impact of unionization on the
development of workers' identity and employer-employee relations.

Finally, from a political perspective, it was widely known that Metal
Empresa was linked to an important leftist party, Vanguardia Revolucionaria (VR).[2] Some of the best leaders of Vanguardia became agitators
and organizers at Metal Empresa. The principal union leaders of Metal
Empresa became party activists or at least accepted the influence of Vanguardia. These leaders were widely known in the union movement of
the 1970s because of their role in coordinating the unions that were pro-
Vanguardia.

To come to grips with the complicated reality that I proposed to analyze, I designed a set of specific questions that encompassed the central
concerns of the research. I prepared a chronology of the union's history
and arranged for preliminary interviews. I used these exploratory, open-
ended interviews to test the specific questions that were subsequently used
in more in-depth interviews. This background work and a review of the
union's files helped me to establish the main demographic characteristics
of the company's workers (i.e., age, qualifications, and birthplace) and
establish the criteria for selecting my interviewees.

I conducted in-depth interviews with nine workers. Five of these had
never been union leaders and four had some experience as union leaders.
Five were serranos (i.e., persons from the interior highland provinces of
Peru) and four were *criollos* (i.e., persons from coastal Peru). Five of my
interviewees could be classified as "highly skilled" workers while four
were "mostly unskilled." The group included four boilermakers, three
blowtorch operators, and one welder. The composition of this original
group of interviewees did not reflect the demographic makeup of Metal
Empresa's workforce as a whole. It was impossible to assemble a representative sample because of the reluctance of many workers to be interviewed, although the original group of nine interviewees did help establish the principal lines that divided and differentiated workers.

I was able to compensate for the lack of a representative sample in my
in-depth interviews by doing a wider range of interviewing in the factory

on certain selected topics. I asked twenty current or former workers of Metal Empresa to provide information in individual interviews or group discussions. Topics included the problems of unions, the differences in unions across trades, the relations of unions with leftist parties, and the involvement of workers in economic activities outside of the factory. In this way, I added to my knowledge about welders, for example, who were underrepresented in my interview pool.

I am grateful for the cooperation of all the workers who told me their stories between May and September 1984. The information from and opinions of the following people made this work possible: Pedro Aguirre, Daniel Angulo, Justiniano Bautista, Miguel Calle, Timoteo Calvo, Luciano Castillo, Máximo Chinga, Enrique Condori, Roberto Díaz, Ramón Espinoza, Luis Helfers, Carlos Hidalgo, Gerardo Iraita, Máximo Julca, Robinson Ledesma, Antonio Miguel Lescano, Tomás Licona, Freddy Llamoca, Rolando Luzquiño, Orestes Merino, Jorge Murriagui, Feliciano Pacheco, Celestino Peralta, Pedro Pizarro, Delmer Quiroz, Conrado Reyes, Vidal Ricapa, Evaristo Sales, Bartolomé Valverde, César Vásquez, Braulio Vega, Esteban Vilcahuamán, Oscar Zelada, and Jesús Zúñiga Sotomayor. I remember each one I met as I did the interviews. Some took place in my office (where some of the men were kind enough to come), others in the privacy of their homes, others at the union offices. Another round of interviews took place in the union auditorium during the strike they carried out in 1984. During the strike, these men not only helped me with my research but invited me to share meals with them at the union's soup kitchen. It would be difficult to forget their sincerity, their lucid perceptions, and the strength of their convictions. That strength will be evident to readers. I fondly remember Conrado Reyes's request: "I'd like for you to continue to be concerned about the workers even if you never come back to the factory." That concern, in part, was what prompted the company to file a complaint against me with the Callao police department when I was doing the research.

Before conducting the interviews with the company workers, I did interviews with the leaders of the metallurgical unions. The interviews with Jaime Cáceres, Angel Gallardo, Walter Huatuco, and Emilio Hazaña were very useful. There were also interviews with Jaime Donayre from the Federación de Trabajadores de la Industria de Papeles, with Orestes Rodríguez, a worker from Moraveco, with Carlos Torres, a worker from Toyota, and with Guillermo Castro from the Centro de Investigación, Estudios y Documentación (CIED). During the course of my research, I also interviewed some left-wing party activists who had done their political work with workers from Metal Empresa. They also gave me access to their documents.

This book has three parts. The first part examines the social meaning of working-class life through the experience of workers at Metal Empresa. I look at workers' initial aspirations when they entered the factory and the power relations that unfolded in the factory. The analysis moves on to consider how unionization modified the relationships between workers and company management, the nexus between political and trade union activism, and the limitations on the company's ability to create an integrated, stable workforce. Finally, our attention will turn to how workers dealt with Peru's economic crisis. These topics are taken up again in the second part of the book in the oral history of Jesús Zúñiga Sotomayor, a former worker for Metal Empresa. His autobiography gives us an in-depth insider's view. He is a man who knows how to and likes to communicate. He offers us insights about his childhood in the sierra, his move to Lima, his political activism, his independent activity as a small-scale entrepreneur, and his efforts on behalf of his province. It is a story told by a multidimensional man who transformed his life many times, from that of an Andean shepherd to that of a small businessman in the capital. The last part of the book synthesizes the main arguments of this research.

This study was prepared and written with the support of the Instituto de Estudios Peruanos (IEP). I must acknowledge my special debt to Julio Cotler. He invited me to carry out a study of workers as part of the Instituto's project "Urbanization and Popular Urban Classes" sponsored by the Inter-American Foundation. I thank Julio for his insightful suggestions and personal encouragement. The former director of the Instituto, José Matos Mar, openly encouraged me from the start and always ensured that I had the material support that I needed to carry out the study. I also owe a debt to our working group of researchers on urban wages made up of Pedro Galín, Julio Carrión, and Oscar Castillo. In the course of my continuous exchange of ideas with them, I developed the lines of inquiry pursued in this study. I appreciate the encouragement I received from them and from Jürgen Golte, María Rostworoski, Norma Adams, Nicolás Lynch, Cecilia Blondet, Marisol de la Cadena, and all my friends at the Instituto.

I am grateful for the intelligent and dedicated research assistance of

Jorge Villón, a former worker and union leader of Metal Empresa. In numerous and lengthy conversations, we reflected on working-class life. I am grateful to Luis Pásara, director of our Centro de Estudios de Derecho y Sociedad (CEDYS), a friend who frequently listened and took a lively interest in the progress of the research. My gratitude also extends to Julio Cotler, Alberto Flores Galindo, Luis Pásara, Gonzalo Portocarrero, Guillermo Rochabrún, and Jorge Villón for contributing their very helpful reflections, suggestions, and criticism. Their comments helped to improve the final draft of the book and even suggested new avenues for continued research.

I am grateful to Señora Violeta Ramos of the Office of IEP for her care and concern and to Señora Anna Collantes, Señora Aída Nagata, Señora María Angélica Velásquez, and Señora Elizabeth Andrade for their patient and meticulous work in transcribing my recorded interviews and for typing the drafts.

1

Becoming a Factory Worker

Becoming a factory worker during the 1960s and 1970s—especially a skilled and steadily employed factory worker, like those of Metal Empresa—was an aspiration among the *sectores populares* of Lima. People without stable employment, unskilled laborers, and those with jobs that required heavy physical labor viewed the factory as a place to secure a better-paying job. In the factory, a person could learn new skills and enhance his future prospects in the labor market. Following the enactment of new labor laws in 1970, a factory job also meant that workers could expect job security.

Many provincial migrants came to Lima with high expectations about the opportunities to be found in factory jobs. They would start out as low-paid, unskilled laborers with workdays that lasted well beyond eight hours. They took jobs in small businesses and shops and received wages that barely covered their living expenses. The factory workers in Metal Empresa started out in such jobs. Before coming to Metal Empresa, some had been sidewalk food vendors. Others worked as stock boys in hardware stores or warehouses. A few worked as apprentices in auto body shops.

After spending some time in their first jobs, some workers sought out the relatively higher wages offered at the time in the construction industry. Others went to learn an industrial trade in a workshop or went to work directly for a company. Learning a trade meant progress for a migrant in his quest to incorporate himself into city life. To Feliciano Pacheco, who worked in a warehouse at the time, becoming a mechanic meant attaining "a higher paid profession, one in higher demand, since a mechanic was looked upon differently than a waiter, a butler, or a warehouse worker." Therefore, he naturally "was anxious to become a mechanic." In the long run, learning a trade would offer him a chance for a better income and a job that was less physically demanding. Other benefits were also associated with becoming a skilled worker. You would be in a better position to look for other jobs, especially if you could get one in a larger company. Such jobs were thought to be more prestigious. Such a job could make it possible to save some money and open up a small business of your own. With these expectations in mind, large numbers of provincial people migrated to Lima and sought employment in industry. Migrants surpassed the number of Lima-born workers. For example, 85 percent of the workers of Metal Empresa in 1984 came from the provinces. Of a total of 171 workers, only 27 had been born in the cities of Lima and Callao. Every day, year after year, workers from at least nineteen of the different departments of Peru met at the plant to work, to make demands on their employers, and to become friends.[1]

The migrants who left temporary and unskilled jobs to become factory workers generally met certain minimal educational requirements that made them eligible to take on skilled jobs. Some had an elementary school education from their hometown. But many workers completed elementary school by attending night school in Lima. This added to their day's workload. Grade school was not just a formal requirement for factory work but was seen by the workers as a means to become more competitive on the job. This was the attitude of Freddy Llamoca, who, despite having finished grade school in his hometown, enrolled again in the third grade in Lima. He explained, "I saw myself as somewhat less prepared; it seems like education in the provinces is very different so then I began to go back to school."

In any case, migrants needed to meet certain requirements to get their personal identification documents, which were indispensable for obtaining work in a company. For example, Braulio Vega spent two years as a clerk in a hardware store while waiting to get his military inscription papers so that he could apply for factory jobs.

Relatives and friends who had moved from the provinces to Lima played a critical role in encouraging new migrants to seek jobs in industry. They provided information about employment opportunities, they gave advice, and sometimes they explicitly pressured their relatives to apply for factory jobs. Jesús Zúñiga left a public works construction job in 1968 for industrial work, even though the job paid less. According to Jesús, he did so "because of the advice my brother-in-law gave me, who said I wouldn't learn anything, that it would be better to go into metallurgical workshop than to study at night and that I could learn to do welding and soldering, boilermaking, blueprint reading, and because it wouldn't be as tough a job as construction work. I paid attention to him because he was so concerned

TABLE I. *Metal Empresa Workers by Department of Origin, 1984*

Department	Number of Workers
Ancash	12
Apurímac	7
Arequipa	12
Ayacucho	5
Cajamarca	7
Callao	14
Cerro de Pasco	3
Cusco	2
Huancavelica	5
Huánuco	2
Junín	6
La Libertad	7
Lambayeque	8
Lima	24 (City: 13)
Loreto	1
Moquegua	1
Piura	43 (Talara: 22)
Puno	8
Tumbes	1
Unidentified	2
City of Lima and Callao:	27
Migrants from the coast	47
Migrants from the sierra	56
Migrants from the jungle	1
Unidentified origin	14

Source: Data provided by the union.

that I would be stuck in construction." Sometimes people from a province would counsel their compatriots about jobs even before they arrived in the city. Thanks to information from several migrants returning from Lima, Conrado Reyes left Marcavelica in Sullana province and arrived in Lima with an astonishingly clear objective: to learn the boilermaker's and welder's trade in the metallurgical industry. With this goal and with information he got from a buddy from his province, Reyes found work as an apprentice in boilermaking and welding at Labarthe Shipyards a few months after arriving in Lima.

Relatives and people from the countryside not only directed the recently arrived migrant with information but also would help him get into a workshop by recommending him to management. When seeking a factory job, many provincials looked to brothers-in-law, cousins, or pals from the province to intercede on their behalf. Thus it was not surprising to find many migrants from the same province in a single factory. A large number of *talareños* who got hired by Metal Empresa early on did so with the help of the personnel manager, who was from the same province. Even though many had already left the company by 1984, there was still a group of 22 talareños out of a total of 171 workers. Any worker who had close ties with the bosses would use this connection to recommend his fellow provincials, relatives, and close associates for job openings.

Without this personal direction and support from someone inside the factory, getting settled in an industrial job was difficult. It might require long training periods or involve being shifted around constantly as an unskilled laborer. One example is the case of Percy Hinojosa, who did not have "anyone to guide him." After an endless string of less desirable jobs, he finally got a steady factory job after twelve years in Lima. His effort to succeed, illustrated in his journey through the labor market, also underscores how profoundly important landing a steady industrial job could be for a migrant.

The abject poverty in which his family lived after his father's death forced Percy Hinojosa to leave home. He left his mother and younger siblings behind to take care of the animals on the family farm in a mountainside community. He was fifteen years old when he arrived in Lima. His goal was to educate himself. To do so, he got a job as a domestic servant for a family while enrolling in a night school. After two years, Percy left the servant's job. "I realized it wasn't right for me," he explained. Then, he began to work. He described winding his way from factory to factory:

> I worked at Coca-Cola, at Cuadernos Atlas, and in the Italian bakery. Later on, I would work at Pepsi-Cola, in small shops, in furniture factories, and carpentry shops. I would work two months and a half or three and I'd be laid off. I think the companies didn't want you to have a steady job at that time. In the companies I'd help the workers who had steady jobs, those who already had positions. For example, at Coca-Cola I'd help in bottle control, in counting and selecting bottles. At Cuadernos Atlas also, I'd pack the notebooks, different kinds with fifty or one hundred sheets or those which were lined or

had squares by the dozen. In the furniture shops, I'd help sandpaper according to the instructions that the craftsmen would give me.

Percy was relatively satisfied: "At that time, there was at least a possibility that you'd have work; things were easier although you wouldn't earn much, things didn't cost so much, and you could eat at that time for less than five soles, with a choice of the daily specials. Then if you made twenty soles it was enough to get by. Of course, you couldn't find a steady job."

But after a couple of years in different companies, Percy became convinced that he "couldn't go on this way either" and that he naturally wanted to "learn a trade, even if it was as a carpenter, because whatever I learn in a few days as a temporary worker doesn't get me anywhere because a few days later I'm working somewhere else, right?" He gave another reason why he sought job security: "I didn't want to go on wandering from one job to another. Each time you got a new job, you had to seek job clearance from the police station showing that you had no previous criminal record. The clearance was valid for only sixty days, or for thirty days. And you had to get them because they were required." Finally, he wanted a better wage: "I'd earn little and my brothers were still back there in the countryside and I'd like to help them sometimes and I'd help with what I could but it wasn't enough. That's why I got into construction work for about four years because there you did earn well."

At the age of nineteen, Percy became a construction worker and labored on different projects earning more than in his earlier jobs and learning the carpenter's trade. Although in construction he enjoyed greater job security than before, he felt unhappy about the frequent layoffs in the trade. He decided: "It wasn't feasible to stick with it because sometimes I'd work for two months, a month, or a year, but once I finished the job, I'd have to go back waiting around until another project might turn up for a month or a couple of weeks. Thus you had to, whether you wanted to or not, get involved in small construction jobs with a new contractor or something else like that." Besides, being a construction worker kept him from achieving his original purpose in coming to Lima, which was to educate himself and learn a trade. He explained: "I had to drop out of school. Sometimes, they sent you out to work at another site, for example, to Monterrico, San Borja, or Chaclacayo, and this didn't give me enough time to study at night in high school. For example, from Chaclacayo I'd have to come up to Neighbor Unit #3, near where I was studying, but I'd get there around eight o'clock at night and I was forced to give up studying."

Percy got into an automobile repair shop as an apprentice mechanic. He began to learn the trade and after a while was given jobs to do on his own. Given his new responsibilities, he decided to ask for a pay raise, but the shop owner turned him down. Then Percy discovered something new: to better himself he needed to be less submissive and find some way to stand up to the owner. First, he sought to negotiate: "Since the owner refused to give me a raise, we made a deal. Many times you have to work late in the shop, so then I proposed my own schedule working from such and such an hour for eight hours and he accepted it." But the owner did not keep his part of the bargain and he made Percy stay late to finish parking cars. Percy then decided to complain. He argued with the owner and criticized him in front of his fellow workers. As Percy put it,

> You can't bow your head and just go on working. There were so many places that were unionizing. . . . Even though I didn't know what a union was, right? I wanted to have my rights respected, too. However, some co-workers at the mechanics shop were painters and clothes pressers. They were not like me. They just wanted to work. They were afraid when they saw me arguing. Then I think the owner realized what I was doing. One day he told me I was dangerous because I was leading his workers. Suddenly got the idea that I'd set up something like a union and I still didn't know what a union was or whether or not it was easy or hard to organize one. Okay, so then he told me to submit my resignation and I did so and went back to my home in the countryside.

Percy stayed at home for about a year. When he returned in 1973, he discovered that it was even more difficult to get a job. A friend who was working in Moraveco (an appliance factory) tried to help him. He spoke to one of his relatives who was an office worker in the company so that Percy might get in. But Percy refused. After twelve years in Lima, he dreamed of something better and wanted job security as well as good wages. His experience at the auto body shop had made him savvy about working conditions. He knew that "the work in Moraveco was very basic and tough and they didn't provide good working conditions, not even gloves or clothing." Then he sought out the family for which he had been a domestic servant when he first came to Lima. The son in the family was an employee of Metal Empresa. He did Percy a favor by recommending him for employment.

But this rough road, like that trod by many others who flocked to the factories, did not end when Percy got work. Soon after he was hired the workers of Metal Empresa began demanding job security. Before the Law of Security of Employment of 1970, job security simply meant that one had to avoid getting fired. After the enactment of the law, attaining job security involved a formal procedure through which one could gain official status as "stable" worker. Once a worker had this status, it was very difficult for an employer to fire him. Acquiring this status required making it through a probationary period of three months that was prescribed by law.

The goal of workers was to liberate themselves from the uncertainty in which they lived by securing this new legal protection. The enthusiasm that workers displayed when the law was enacted showed how meaningful it was to them. "When it [the law] was made public," Jesús Zúñiga recalled, "all the workers under contract celebrated in the factory and there were workers who exclaimed, what the hell, I've got a steady job! People were embracing and shouting behind the tanks. There were even a few who were crying. . . . Everyone let go of all that pent-up emotion and they put up signs in the bathrooms and in the locker rooms."

The intense drive to acquire job security was also apparent among those who were hired after the promulgation of the law. To pass the probationary period, some workers staged accidents in which they were injured. By being on medical leave, they could not be fired according to law. "I asked a co-worker to burn my arm with a blowtorch," Alberto Ruiz told me, "other workers threw themselves out of the boat from above while others anesthetized their fingers with Coranine and hammered them." "I staged an on-the-job accident by burning my own hand," Fred Llanos related, "that's how I got in three months and they couldn't let me go. I still have the scar."

Job security, however, was contingent on the approval of management. Managers decided who would stay and who would not. That meant job security involved competing with fellow workers.

One of the advantages that workers born in Lima enjoyed was a better education. When Luis Helfers started at Metal Empresa, he recalled seeing "the boilermakers doing their tracing and sketches of front and profile views." He discovered that the technical drawing which he had studied so indifferently in school helped him. Some workers even went through technical training before coming to work. In contrast to the difficulties that recent migrants faced, a limeño like Daniel Angulo could take advantage of connections and information to get this kind of training early on. While in school, he sought a scholarship given by an industrial firm. He studied at Servicio Nacional de Adiestramiento en Trabajo Industrial (SENATI—National Industrial Training Service), where he was trained in building metal structures. Rather than view his job search as something strictly linked to one's qualifications, a limeño was apt to go job hunting where he might get better wages. He moved from one factory to another depending on where the opportunities were.

But in addition, to win over the bosses, the worker from Lima would use his ability to strike up personal connections with them. Angulo recalled how he secured his job: "I used to play soccer then and there was going to be a championship game between teams from the industrial communities of the factories and the coach of the team told me not to worry, that I would get my permanent job because they needed me." Naturally, the criollo's advantage in interpersonal relations was viewed as suspect by the serranos. "The Lima native," remarked Feliciano Pacheco, "thinks of ways to ingratiate himself with the boss. More often than not, he's looking for a chance to have a couple of drinks with the boss on Saturday or uses other ways like always saying 'hi' to him and expecting to get something back in return." On the other hand, the migrant, especially one from the Andes, makes use of his main personal resource: his willingness to work. According to Jesús Zúñiga, serranos were accustomed to hard work since childhood. He proudly noted that their characteristic trait is that "the serranos don't suck up; they get out in front and face the problems that come their way." That is why a serrrano worker like Esteban Vilcahuamán bragged about having obtained job security "just by working and working humbly, standing up and showing work and effort." That industriousness also let him qualify on the job and compensate for his inferior education. At the same time, the serrano was more submissive before authority. "You would give it your all without stopping, whatever were the bosses' demands," Jesús Zúñiga remembered, "whoever went into a place of employment just kept his head down and that was that."

Their dedication and obedience evoked anger on the part of limeño workers, who resented the migrants' competition for positions or over-time. Their presence made limeños feel uncomfortable because, as Luis Pretell confessed:

> We're not lovers of work. Have you ever heard the Cuban song that God made work as a punishment? Sometimes it would be said jok-ingly, "Are we 'clasista workers?' No, we're only clasistas!" Hard workers are jerks. No criollo is going to say that he doesn't like work but that's the truth. Although what happens is that the criollo doesn't like to work as much as the serrano. He's not a jerk. The criollo has his own work pace and says, "I work according to how they pay me." The criollo has skills and wants maximum compensation. He wants to get more with minimum effort. He knows that the owners appro-priate the surplus value. So some would say crap to us like, "I already worked an hour to pay for my wage, the rest is for the employer." But the serrano is different. Whether they pay him well or not, he always works just the same. He's ready to break his back and bow his head. He works like a busy bee. They would always give the toughest jobs to them. Whoever comes from the sierra necessarily starts out as a helper. He starts at the bottom and does no matter what it takes to watch and learn and work his ass off. He learns and he's always taking shit. Because damn, if sheet metal has to be moved and the crane isn't working, he grabs it or ties it to his waist and then tugs it like a burro. Then he takes it to its place so that the boilermaker over there might mark and trace it and again he goes back pulling or carrying it on his back or over his knee or cut into sections. Anyone else would not do such a stupid thing. Isn't there a crane or somebody to carry the sheet? What do I do now? I'm a boilermaker, not a person who's supposed to carry a heavy load on my back. If you want somebody to do that, look for them at La Parada [a market where the unemployed gather]. The worker from Lima replies, "Well that's it!" And if the engineer comes to stop you, you throw down your hammer and square and all your crap and go to the rest room. The serrano won't do that. The engineer will stop him and he goes running to bring a rope and breaks his ass, dripping with sweat like a horse. He likes work because he's being controlled.

Workers from Lima felt that they were on the losing end because of the availability of large numbers of these hardworking men from the provinces who flooded the job market. Limeños saw serranos as limiting their opportunities for employment, driving down wages, and, in some cases, even displacing them from their jobs. For a worker from Lima like Luis Pretell, the serranos came "to ruin the market; they're the ones who messed it up, of course. You can't believe how they cheapen themselves. They come and take orders at any price and they take any wage. Then when a qualified person shows up they slam the door in his face. That's what the employers want: the kind of people who'll work their butts off for two soles." Luis Pretell's complaint was not gratuitous: he lost a job in a newspaper and was replaced by two serranos. He recalled his experience: "I had two serrano assistants and every day it was the same stupidity. Bring the paper over here, and look this is how it's done. The cholo learned the setup. The year was over and the bosses said to me, 'You know, that's all we need you for.' The cholos had learned and now knew how to do everything I did. I had taught them so that they might help me then, not to dump on me. The serranos were kept on and that's what happens. The serrano learns a little crap and there he stays."

These attitudinal differences did not cause serious conflicts among the workers. But there were personal clashes, generally diluted by the criollos' good humor and the inscrutability of the serranos. The attitude of the serranos toward work was criticized by the criollos as being purely mechanical and physical. Criollos made their point "by saying that we [serranos] were all animals or beasts," Esteban Vilcahuamán related. And indeed, as a way of justifying the verbal attacks on serranos, Luis Pretell explained: "The serrano kills himself every day, he doesn't even have time to take a crap. He works his butt off all day and he hardly develops his brain. But all day long, he's moving his arms, shaking his ass, because he's working. The engineer, the personnel manager, or the supervisor, never see him thinking because all day he has a tool in his hand; all day he's busting his butt, but his brain doesn't function; he's acting mechanically." At times, his own ethnic identity would be hurled at him by the criollos in the form of an insult: Serrano!

But the serranos had plenty of reasons for not feeling overly uncomfortable because they knew that their fate depended on the fact that they were excellent machinists. They kept their cool because they realized that "the bosses already know that for a tough or difficult job they could mainly call on the provincial people," as Feliciano Pacheco said. This knowledge gave them a feeling of superiority vis-à-vis the criollos and provided psychological comfort that protected them from attacks. "The people from Lima would throw out the label, serrano," Esteban Vilcahuamán noted, "but when we were working, it didn't matter to us. When they called me an animal or a beast, I'd thank them. Thanks, I'd say to them, because I'm not a beast or a brute either. Because if I were a beast, I wouldn't be able to climb that wall or hang myself from a rope and calmly solder and cut while you can't do it."

In fact, the serranos looked down on the criollos. They believed the criollo compañeros were scared of physical labor, taking the easiest and lightest jobs and leaving the heavy ones to the serranos. Feliciano Pacheco explained: "The boilermaker's job is very hard, especially at the height of summer when the sun is beating down. When we work inside the tanks, the heat goes through the sheet metal and we're cutting and welding inside. It's practically like a sauna bath. You sweat like a horse in there and that scares a limeño away from the job. On the other hand, a serrano hangs right in there."

To the serrano, the criollo is lazy and "a shirker" besides. In other words, "a criollo would act like he was working when he was doing something else." Jesús Zúñiga explained, "If we're going to carry a table among several people, the guy from Lima acts like he's carrying it but he isn't holding up his end." So the serranos also found reason to return the disdain that the criollos heaped on them. Serranos made fun of criollos and implied that they were wimps because "they'd get tired and leave the work for the next day," or "they'd look for gloves for their hands." Serranos scorned criollos because "they thought they were smart, but it's all bootlicking and fast talking and nothing more." As one put it, "They're going nowhere fast."

Serranos found their Andean ancestry to be a source of pride, not shame. According to Jesús Zúñiga, they understood the limeños to be lazy "because of the environment itself, because he hasn't gotten up at three in the morning to herd cattle or carry firewood." In the view of Esteban Vilcahuamán, "We, the serranos, are smarter than the criollos and we have nerves of steel because we were raised in the mountains, amid the hills, in rain, in the elements, in mud, in huts, and in the midst of landslides. Perhaps we are accustomed to suffering hunger and misery, so for us going to work is not so hard. On the contrary, it's easy."

Animated by their own reflections on the subject, several serranos went even further to underscore their pride in their Andean ancestry, history,

architecture, and even their physical appearance. Thus Esteban Vilcahuamán proudly proclaimed:

> They're the animals; they're the beasts. Of course I'm a serrano! I'm
> a serrano through my ancestry. I'd like to say to some criollos, have
> you seen the scientific advances in the world? I'd like you to tell me
> what scientist can operate on a skull with a stone? What scientist has
> there been who can build a building with pure brute strength, with-
> out water? You've never seen at any time nor heard of the building
> the Incas did here in Cuzco and elsewhere in Cajamarca, the *pongo,*
> the springs; you haven't heard of anything like those hillside irriga-
> tion canals? Have you heard of anything like it? Then, when you call
> me a serrano you're recognizing that I'm truly one of their children,
> the great-grandson of those scientists. Or maybe that I'm a son of
> the Incas. No kidding, really. Fine, my color isn't exactly right, but
> that's because of the stain we have, the crossbreeding, because truly
> the crossbreeding has stained everything. But I still have the face. I'm
> a serrano. I'm clean shaven. I still have the face with the high cheek-
> bones. I'd give it right back to the criollos. Then, whenever they'd
> say "serrano" to me, they'd then say, "Damn it, there's no use arguing
> with this guy because he's one tough serrano."

In any case, the differences between criollos and serranos at work are
better understood if the social circumstances surrounding their decisions
to seek factory work are considered. While the migrant seeks industrial
employment in order to get ahead socially, the limeño is almost always
somebody who became a worker because he couldn't get ahead. "My
father," Gerardo Contreras observed, "never thought I was going to end
up this way as a worker because his goal was that I go up the ladder. He
hoped that I might be higher than him." The serrano arrives at the factory having thought about the future. The criollo is there because he did
not think about the future. As Eduardo Sotelo admitted: "I didn't think
about the future and I didn't have anybody to give me advice and guide
me during my adolescence."

The Lima native is apt to feel that he has not taken advantage of the
educational resources of the city to secure better employment: "I studied
until the middle of the third year of secondary school," Freddy Llanos related. "I didn't finish because they kicked me out of high school. I mis-
behaved and I shouldn't have. I was the school prankster who kept bad

company. With maturity you come to see things in a more realistic way. What I have lost is time that I should have taken advantage of and then I'd have been in a better position." In this case as in others, the criollo always feels that "he could have been something else, that he could have taken another road. For example, I'd have liked to become a doctor," Sotelo told me.

In the recollections of a limeño, there are always events and circumstances that should have turned out differently. If Pretell's father had not died so soon, if Llanos had not been kicked out of high school, if Sotelo had somebody to guide him. Last, Luis Pretell joked, "If there had been work as a manager, I'd have been a manager."

For the worker from the provinces, undertaking manual labor in a factory is evidence of his progress, and he values it. "The work of boiler-making is linked to metals and it's a fascinating job for me," Feliciano Pacheco said, "because each job has its own characteristics, it isn't monotonous or repetitive; it's completely different. Boilermaking is such a big field that I never stop learning. Working in metallurgy makes me feel like an accomplished professional." Feliciano Pacheco even spurned an offer to become an employee working in drafting. "I asked what the job was like and they explained to me that it was doing some kinds of drawings in the office. Fine, and that I wasn't going to learn anything else and I wouldn't go any higher. On the other hand, working in boilermaking, I was going to work in the plant and with each job you learn more."

In contrast, many people from Lima dream about making up for lost time by moving up to be an office employee. "If you can you might get to be a manager," fantasized Contreras. "At the very least," Pretell said, he'd "like to be a clerk in order to screw around and receive a salary, supervise, check out everything, surrounded by very nice women with good figures who are going to screw around, too." His complaint is that "the employers unfortunately don't look at it this way." For a limeño, manual labor is proof of his stagnation. When a limeño goes to work, Pretell says, "he feels like he's going to a concentration camp."

2

Standing Up for Yourself as a Worker

Once inside the factory, workers came face-to-face with the logic of Peruvian business. Beyond the factory gates, the behavior of business was shaped by the market. Inside the factory, management controlled the labor force by resorting to despotic treatment. As former union leader Delmer Quiroz put it, management treated workers in the same way that a foreman on a traditional hacienda treated peasants.[1]

Metal Empresa was founded in 1968 after the bankruptcy of an earlier enterprise, Promecán. Some of the Promecán stockholders invested in the new company. It was devoted to the production of capital goods for other industries, mainly metal fishing boats, boilers, metal structures, and containers. The company, like all those that manufacture metal products, depended heavily on manual labor. The manufacturing process involved transforming sheet metal and beams into pieces that were then assembled into large size products. The workers participated in teams that carried out different specialized tasks: tracing the designs on sheet metal, cutting and welding the sheets, following the plans and instructions of the engineers. Metallurgical production of this type can be only partially mechanized. A company's productivity depends largely on the skills of manual labor.

During the early years of Metal Empresa, the educational qualifications of the workers were minimal. The company's production was based on the gross physical exploitation of workers. In great measure, the profitability of the firm depended on organizing time-efficient work shifts and expanding and intensifying those shifts. To make the shift as productive as possible, the company strictly enforced the eight-hour work schedule, making sure that there was no slack time. The company did not permit workers to arrive late, even by a minute or two. Workers who lived in squatter settlements outside of the city complained about how early they had to leave home to arrive punctually for the seven-thirty morning whistle. It was the same at quitting time. Workers were permitted to put down their tools, get cleaned up, and change clothes only after the whistle blew at the end of the workday. Of course, the half hour interruption for lunch was not counted as part of the eight-hour workday.

At the same time, the company zealously monitored working time inside the factory. Visits from family members were not allowed, not even to leave a brief message. Workers could not interrupt work to make telephone calls. Informal conversation between workers was prohibited, and time to go to the rest room was strictly monitored. As workers used to say, you had to work from "whistle to whistle." Furthermore, to increase the work pace (by cutting down the time devoted to performing each discrete task and in so doing increasing production), the group leaders pressured the workers in their sections to speed up completion of their jobs.[2] Sometimes they insulted them by calling them fools and imbeciles if they did not work up to speed. Finally, to expand the workday to keep up with orders, the company contracted workers for overtime shifts that paid better than the usual hourly rate for the shift.

A system of penalties, which included warnings, suspensions, and firings, guaranteed that all the restrictions and controls set up by the company to maximize efficiency functioned. The system reinforced the authority of those in charge of monitoring of workers in different sections of the plant on a daily basis. According to workers, sanctions were often applied arbitrarily. The workers would even be punished if they argued and, of course, if they talked back in response to the verbal attack of a group leader. In this period in the plant, work was described by some as "slavery."

The company safeguarded its profits by limiting labor costs. It kept wages low. It also avoided expenditures to improve working conditions and kept the wage advances that workers could request during times of need to a minimum. The company offered only minimal wage increases. It made workers pay for their own overalls and shoes and did not supply paper towels or toilet paper. There was no in-house cafeteria. Workers hurriedly ate their lunches at kiosks on the street between shifts. Despite frequent on-the-job accidents, there was no medical assistance. Workers could expect only minimal loans for extraordinary expenses such as the birth of a child or sickness or death of a family member. The company's generally unsympathetic response to calamities like a death in the family generated great resentment among workers. "When my wife died," a worker recalled, "I said to the personnel manager, sir, I need a loan, give me something. He told me that I had only been there for two and a half months and couldn't ask for a loan. Then he just turned around from behind a table and laughed brazenly."

Controlling workers' hours, as much as limiting wages, was a way to assure profits. The system rested on a basic condition which the company cultivated: keeping its relations with its workers on an individual basis. The relations between workers and the company were not uniform but varied from one individual to another, based on each worker's individually signed contract. The contract was temporary and subject to renewal every few months. Whatever problem or interchange between the worker and the company authorities, whether it was about a pay hike, a loan, a day off, a disciplinary problem, or workloads, was an individual matter. Whether the issue was handled by the personnel manager or group leader, the boss always had the final say. This setup made it easy to limit pay raises and impose discipline on the workers. At contract renewal time, the company would decide unilaterally what the total amount of a wage increase would be, that is, if it deemed one was deserved. If the worker asked for a raise or argued for an increase larger than he was given, the company could flatly reject the appeal. The typical response by the company was that there was a surplus of workers on the job market. One worker recalled being told, "If you don't agree, the door is wide open over there and if you're a troublemaker you can leave. Look how things are outside; you quit and somebody else gets hired. There's no problem." The grim reality of the labor market was the best guarantee of labor discipline. Workers knew that if they did not give in on their contract, it would not be renewed. So "people just put up with it."

Keeping relations between the company and the workers on a one-to-one basis was the top priority of the firm. It was clear that a union would establish the right of workers to bargain collectively on wage increases and other matters. A union would make it hard to keep down labor costs. Obviously, it was advantageous to the company to prevent the formation of a union. Toward this end, the company took advantage of the situation to create ties of personal dependence and guarantee the loyalty of a group of workers by granting them individual favors and concessions. In exchange for these privileges, workers cooperated and informed the company on attempts at union organizing.

The personnel manager organized a group known in the factory as the *argolla* (ring). He mainly favored his fellow talareños. The manager's favored workers would be assigned to be group leaders. In turn, group leaders placed their relatives in the best jobs. This practice benefited the plant workers who were their friends and from the same provinces. As a result, talareño workers who were in a lower job category would end up earning more than those in higher ones. Inversely, workers who were not in the argolla but who were more skilled were contracted and categorized as assistants in order to perform jobs in their specialty. Preferential treatment was also evident in job assignments. One worker related that, for example, when a section leader delegated jobs to his group leader, the latter, "who was a relative of the personnel manager's brother-in-law," would give the lightest jobs to his buddies. They also received privileges that other workers did not enjoy. Members of the argolla got permission to go to the medical clinic and their time off would not be deducted from their extra Sunday pay, as it was for others. Managers tolerated tardiness among these workers. Even if they did not show up at work on time, their time cards would be punched as if they had.

The privileged workers returned the favors to the managers by giving them gifts from time to time—a bottle of whiskey, a turkey, or a chicken. In addition, they might invite the personnel manager to some nearby tavern, which helped reinforce the close, personal ties. Workers understood, however, that the most important obligation that was part of their informal pact with management was to safeguard the company's interest on the factory floor. They had to inform management about workers' movements, especially about any attempts to form a union. They also reported acts of misconduct so that fellow workers had to be careful not to be seen resting not only by the bosses but also by these insiders who could turn them in.

The talareños figured out how to take advantage of the situation in their relations with other workers, especially with the serranos, who always were stuck with the toughest jobs. Knowing that most workers lived in fear of the ill will of the personnel manager, the talareños would make fellow workers do work for them by threatening to turn them in for something to the boss. With such a threat hanging over them, workers usually went along. On some occasions, workers were pressured through more delinquent methods: their tools might be hidden or they might be physically impeded from doing their work.

To protect himself and be considered for a raise or an overtime shift, a worker who was not in the argolla had to stay on good terms with the bosses and their friends. One way to do this was to try to work harder on the job and always stay on the good side of a supervisor, foreman, or engineer. This strategy was used especially by serranos. But there was another way to cultivate these relations. Being subjected to intense supervision or receiving overtime hours depended solely on the arbitrary decision of a section or group leader. Those decisions came to be regarded by everyone as personal favors, a kindness extended by the boss that merited a quid pro quo. So, to get ahead, one might give the boss a little gift or invite him out to drink in a local bar or to one of the clandestine bordellos in the area. In turn, the reward for the worker might be some extra time in the rest room or more overtime hours.

Once the union came into existence, a new relationship developed between workers and management. Individual arrangements between workers and bosses gave way to a new system based on the principle that workers' benefits were determined by collective bargaining.

What made this change in the relationship between workers and the company possible? All too frequently in Peru, the analysis of workers' consciousness and behavior has been ignored. It has been viewed as a topic that is intellectually uninteresting or something that can be reduced to the economic calculations made by workers. The prototypical image of workers is one of a "revolutionary proletariat"—but one that has not yet lived up to its revolutionary potential. The real processes that shape the character of the working class have not been examined fully in the Peruvian case.

No matter how brutal the treatment they receive or how impoverished workers might become, neither oppression nor miserable economic conditions in and of themselves explain how workers develop a will to engage in collective action and claim their rights. The experience of oppression by itself was not what made workers see the utility of pursuing their individual aspirations through collective action. What workers had to recognize was that they were all equally affected by the inhumane practices of factory life.

The nature of factory work required cooperation among workers; this made it possible for each worker to realize that his situation was the same as that of his fellow workers. Personal differences aside, they were people who carried out tasks together in the production process; they were all workers. As one serrano put it, despite the unfairness in the allocation of wage increases and the abuses by the argolla of talareños, "the work was one and the same" for everyone without regard to regional and cultural differences. Another recalled the situation this way:

> I'm from the central part of the country. Other workers were from the North or South and we didn't agree about our ideas or lifestyles, like the way some people who got the perks had different ways of doing things. But on the job it was very different. It made no difference there if you were a talareño or from the South or the Center, not at all, just that we were all working together. When we were working on some job, we were all equal because we'd share the same blueprint and if we didn't have a blueprint other workers would pass on a small paper sketch indicating the exact measurements of the pieces that we had to manufacture. When it was time to work, we worked and that's it. There were no differences by party, by province, or because one was from Lima or Callao, nothing like that.

In the process of forming a collective consciousness, it was not enough for workers to recognize that they were equals as producers of material goods. It was also crucial for workers to discover that their shared status —as producers of wealth and, more specifically, profits—cast them into direct conflict with the company. This stage of consciousness developed as workers became aware of how much the company earned and became outraged by the gap between those earnings and their own wages. "We set up the union," a worker declared, "because even though we were filling the company's coffers, they'd charge us for the work clothes they used to give us." As this statement indicates, the worker had reached a critical juncture: he identified himself and his fellow workers as producers of profits with a right to claim a portion. "We've had to demand that they give us clothing," one worker said, "because we are the producers and the ones who truly make the company rich. Because the real situation is very clear to see. They'd earn a large sum of money and they'd give us a lesser amount. See? We came to understand that they were profiting at our expense and exactly for that reason, the company has given us all the benefits it gave us." The character of the metallurgical industry, especially in times of peak production, was such that workers were disposed to compare their wages with profits. In metallurgy, workers participate in every stage of the production of a product. A worker looks at the final product—let's say, a ship—and he knows how many men made it, how many days it took, and how much the men earn. Perhaps this is the reason that metallurgical workers developed a notable tradition of protest and strong union organizations. "I remember vividly when I first came in to work," one worker recalled.

When I started I was earning ninety soles, but they [the company] charged prices in the thousands. We found out how much they charged [for products] through a supervisor and through the businessmen who'd come to sign a contract. This is how we've come to know that we were being very productive and that they [the owners] were getting rich off our sweat while they were paying us the lowest wages they could. Then I came to a conclusion: a job completed in one month, let's say it takes ninety people, then how much is the sum total of wages, and then that left all that money to the company, thousands upon thousands. Then I knew that the company was truly enriching itself with the sweat of our brow. On this basis, we make our demands, because really, damn it, as they say, they're getting out as much as possible from us, so we'll ask for the same.

This consciousness was shared by many workers who had participated in different attempts at union organizing, almost always unsuccessful, in large companies where they had worked before. For example, the migrant serranos who had learned their first skills in small companies did not think of their work as something appropriated by the owners. One worker expressed such a view:

Before, when I used to work in the Compañía del Guano or at the Casa del Freno, what I used to think was that you ought to get ahead by moving up through positions from one company to another. That's what I thought when I saw the companies making progress, right? I also thought about getting together a little capital and starting my own company, I really did. At the Casa del Freno my job wasn't such that I could say that I was making the company rich but rather being there was a help to me. It was more or less like a school for me where they had taught me how to work. That's what I'm referring to. I can't say that the company was getting rich off my sweat. You have to assess things, right? Be fair and realistic.

In small businesses, social differences were veiled by the paternalism of employers. Paternalistic practices cast each worker into a relationship of personal dependency in which the employer's protection and the worker's loyalty create a family atmosphere. The simulation of family life is represented as something that benefits both sides. The establishment of relatively large industrial companies caused a massive expansion of the number of workers in the workplace. With so many workers on the shop floor, paternalistic practices could not be employed effectively to control workers. Big industries tried to use the argolla system to this end, but it ultimately proved to be an ineffective method to control labor.

To ask for a pay raise through a union organization meant much more to workers than just articulating their demands for economic gains. It meant that they were asserting their right to a wage increase and identifying themselves as individuals with rights. Workers understood that their right to a decent wage did not just stem from the fact that they engaged in the backbreaking work of production per se but also because they were producers of profits. The demand for wage increases and the demand that their right to claim wage increases be recognized signified that a working-class identity was finally emerging. Workers saw themselves as equals, as producers of profits, as endowed with rights. To demand a decent wage was to claim an identity that until then had been obscured by dependency relations and the exclusionary practices used by firms. For the workers themselves, the change consisted of ceasing to be treated like "nobodies" so as to be treated "like workers." "When I started out in Metal Empresa," a worker recalled, "we used to have lunch on the street as if we were nobodies because there wasn't a cafeteria. After winning a cafeteria, what we accomplished was that Metal Empresa workers would have lunch like workers, like dignified workers and not like the way they used to treat us."

In order to create and consolidate a union—an alliance of equals—all the diverse components that were part of the social consciousness of workers had to be pulled together and directed toward common objectives. Organizing themselves to act implied, among other things, coming together on a voluntary basis to form a union and collecting signatures on a petition for that purpose, seeking legal recognition of their union by registering with the Ministry of Labor, establishing a system of internal governance and the responsibilities of the leadership, and defining the objectives, mechanisms, and strategies to be used in their dealings with the company. To undertake these tasks, a nascent union needed leaders to encourage and coordinate collective action. Some of the more restless workers had leadership potential, but only one of the workers of

Metal Empresa had any experience in union activities. In the late 1960s and early 1970s, this lack of union experience was not unique among workers in the metallurgical industry. On the contrary, very few workers had any experience of this kind. Frequently, companies harassed unions by blocking their creation and firing workers in the places where they were making inroads in establishing them. According to workers who worked in the metallurgical industry in the 1960s, it was a common practice to dismiss workers and even close down companies altogether after a union was founded. For young migrant workers with little work experience and no familiarity with unions, to launch a union meant giving up one's anonymity as just another factory worker and dealing with government authorities, company experts, and workers who had no background in unions. Under these circumstances, workers needed new kinds of knowledge. On the one hand, they needed information about the mechanisms, deadlines, and paperwork that were legally required for the establishment of the union, its role in negotiations, and rules related to strikes. On the other hand, they also needed to know about ways to deal with the rank and file (e.g., how to lead an assembly or communicate with union members through the union press). In addition, union leaders needed information and the means to prepare themselves to make proposals and take action (e.g., how to decide on what tactics were best to employ, techniques for getting the public's attention about their demands such as distributing flyers and posters).

At the time, however, there was still no institutional network at the national level that workers could call on for help in the process of building unions. Moreover, there was a lack of coverage of union news by the media so workers had little public information with which to work. Finally, workers had qualms about calling on the support of the populist party, APRA (Alianza Popular Revolucionaria Americana). APRA's political involvement in the factories had come to be synonymous with collaboration with the employer. The leaders of workers' groups tied to APRA received special considerations in exchange for colluding with employers. Organizing the masses of workers who dreamed of ending mistreatment and the argolla was supported roundly by the Communist Party, which had long-standing ties to labor and youth groups. The members of the youth group were from the urban middle class. They went to the factories to promote and support the formation of workers' unions. At the same time, they sought political support from the workers for newly created political organizations. These organizations developed into what would be known as *la nueva izquierda* (New Left).

What led educated youths from the urban middle class to seek out the migrant youths who packed Lima's factories? At this juncture, the important, but barely studied, role of middle-class youth in workers' circles requires further comment. The political engagement of students with workers was part of the broader process of social and political change that was taking place in Peru in the 1960s.

Throughout the 1960s, the urban middle class in Peru was the beneficiary of the country's process of modernization. But the children of the middle class found themselves in dilemma. They knew the prosperity enjoyed by their own families in Lima. But it was just as evident that masses of underprivileged people populated the growing slums around the city. The stability of the social order and their own future seemed threatened by the masses, who, by their mere existence, turned Lima into a city besieged by poverty. The slums evoked sharp fears as well as a desire to tap into and channel the poor's feared political potential. But who would offer political vehicles to the poor? The presence of impoverished masses on the urban scene served as a reminder of how the need for change and a commitment to social welfare had been ignored by the traditional political elite. None of the principal political organizations had taken up the cause. For many years, APRA had been toning down its original reformism to make itself more acceptable to an oligarchy that had kept it out of power for thirty years. The new reformism, represented by President Fernando Belaúnde and his Acción Popular (AP), was also showing signs of becoming timid even as Belaúnde tried to conceal the retreat with grandiloquent gestures. The radicalization of youth took place in a context in which the country's need for change seemed obvious. But that need for change was stymied by the absence of a major political actor ready to assume the challenge.

The radicalization process received ideological reinforcement through the doctrinal renewal of the Roman Catholic Church. Starting with the Second Vatican Council in 1964, the church opened up discussions about the problems of the laity and renewed its emphasis on preaching social justice. Little by little, starting with its first cautious statements about social problems, the parameters of the church's social doctrine shifted toward a more radical position that culminated in liberation theology. Liberation theology opened the doors to accepting Marxism as a social science. The youth of the 1960s in Peru and all over Latin America were strongly influenced politically by the Cuban Revolution. The Cuban Revolution, by its very existence, made it possible to envision profound political transformation. A radical interpretation of Christian social thought was espoused by the Colombian priest and guerrilla fighter Camilo Torres.[3] In his life and death, he served as role model who showed that "the duty of a Christian is to be a revolutionary." By leaving behind honors and privileges in Cuba to return to guerrilla warfare in Bolivia, Ernesto "Che" Guevara completed the exhortation to revolution by proclaiming that "the duty of every revolutionary is to make revolutions."[4] Seeing themselves as combatants in a heroic mission to make revolution helped affluent students to deal with the deep-seated guilt that mass poverty evoked in them. One of the radical students later reflected: "Many militants were students who were going to atone for their guilt. In my personal experience, I remember that there was a strong feeling of this kind vis-à-vis the workers. We were incapable of demanding anything from them. We were ready to do whatever it might take, even the smallest things. If the worker couldn't go to a party cell meeting, for example, because he had to take his wife to the movies, it seemed all right to us. But for us personally, it wasn't, hell no. We had years go by without going to the movies."

The political mobilization of these youngsters—who defined themselves as being "to the left" of the Communist Party—took place through the student movement. University students were active in movements that opposed the military regime in the late 1960s. The military government had eliminated citizen participation in elections and in the policymaking process. But the regime also undertook social and economic policies to transform Peru's traditional society. The situation was a bewildering one in Peru's political history. It put radical students in the position of having to define their objections carefully to a government that was politically exclusionary but that was undertaking social reforms. During this period, lengthy writings and political speeches by students were marked by an obsessive need to demonstrate that the military government was not revolutionary even though its bold socioeconomic policies made it seem so. University youth from the Universidad Nacional de Ingeniería (UNI), Universidad Nacional de Agraria, Universidad San Marcos, and Universidad Católica fanned out to the factories to create political bases.

Vanguardia Revolucionaria (VR), a party that eventually established a very active presence among the workers, began its organizing drive in the industrial sector at the end of the 1960s. Four organizations, two of which were universities, were the original bases of VR support: the Federación de Pescadores, the Sindicato de Construcción Civil de Callao, the Universidad Nacional de Ingeniería, and the Universidad Nacional de Agraria. "The students of Vanguardia from the UNI," one militant from that era recalled, "got on a bus that was taking workers to the factories from the Plaza Unión and other places in Lima. From six o'clock in the morning we'd talk to the workers during their ride to work. When we arrived, we'd go back to Plaza Unión and catch another bus." The militant youths also went directly to the factories to get to know workers who were struggling in a disorganized, intuitive way. "We used to be strike-hunters," a militant remembered. "We'd sleep with the workers during the strike; we'd hand out flyers, we'd make posters supporting the strike, and we'd pick up food at the market for them." Many of the contacts with workers were made at the factory doors. Delmer Quiroz, who eventually led union organizing at Metal Empresa, was recruited in this way. "There was chubby guy, Panzer, selling his pamphlets at the factory door," Quiroz would later remember, "and I, very discontented, bought a newspaper. I was reading it closely and a compañero approached me to talk. He asked me what I thought and I gave him my opinion and he asked me if he could talk to me about the main topic in the newspaper and about the political situation in our factory." A few months later, when this inquisitive worker decided to begin organizing a union with the support of the party, he looked to his closest friends at work and, with them, prepared to organize the union. They received advice from a legal consultant provided by VR and a daily assessment from some militant university students. The students helped them by evaluating the development of clandestine activities inside the factory. They advised them specifically on how to deal with the other workers and how to elude being seen by the argolla of talareños. The ongoing assessments of the conditions affecting union organization were largely an intellectual exercise, but they brought together this young, diverse group of activists. The constant engagement of university students in the organizing effort was a notable learning experience for the budding union leaders.

To develop contacts with other workers, the prounion organizing group took advantage of circumstances in its favor. The sheer size of the workforce in the factory made it difficult for management to detect the formation of the prounion movement by relying on the controls provided by the argolla. Among marginalized workers (i.e., those outside of the argolla), a parallel network based on bonds established in the day-to-day work situation, rather than regional or familial ties, could be formed. To obtain the requisite number of signatures that would permit the formation of a union, the prounion group managed secretly to circulate a petition for five months. It was signed by more than half of the workers. In the course of the organizing drive, the prounion workers had to talk workers out of their two main fears about the union. First, they had to assure workers that the union would not betray their confidence and behave like the argolla of talareños. Second, they had to explain to fellow workers that organizing a union would not drive the company into bankruptcy as had been the case with Promecán, the parent firm that preceded Metal Empresa.

Just a few weeks after the union was formed, a new and extremely favorable set of circumstances developed that made it possible to consolidate the union. The Law of Security of Employment of 1970 gave workers a fixed legal right to their jobs in their respective companies. It eradicated the fears that union leaders and the workers who backed them could be summarily dismissed for their activities. The new job security guaranteed stability in union leadership and gave workers confidence in the permanence and continuity of the union itself. Moreover, with the enactment of this law, workers notably increased their ability to negotiate as a union. The new power of the union meant that the company could no longer take advantage of the competition among workers in the labor market to contain workers' demands or depress wages. The company could no longer threaten to fire workers and contract other workers to avoid raises. Finally, the newfound job security heightened the capacity of workers to exert pressure as a union through the use of the strike. Since workers could no longer be replaced, they could use the strike, or at least the threat of a strike, to force the company into negotiations on their demands. Workers took advantage of the strike threat, especially in a period when firms were producing at full capacity and most vulnerable to the losses that labor strife could produce.

The formation of a union reinforced the identity of workers as equals and wage earners with a common bond. Just the creation of the union successfully undermined the implicit threat that organizing to claim workers' rights would lead the company to bankruptcy. That threat had seemed real in light of the history of Promecán, the company that predated Metal Empresa; it was shut down after a union was founded. When it became evident that the establishment of the union would not result in the company filing for bankruptcy, a certain confidence in the company took hold and workers felt a sense of stability.

The union, acting as a new link between the workers and the company, established the equality of all workers in terms of their access to benefits. The union overturned the principle that improvements depended on the personal relations that individual workers maintained with supervisors and company officials. Once the union was functioning, wage increases were granted to all workers in the same way through negotiations based on the list of demands presented by the union. This solidified the sense of unity among workers. It became evident, as one worker said, that "the only way there was to boost wages was by working with the union." In addition to general wage increases, the union negotiated and managed to make available a diverse set of benefits that had been reserved for the protected few such as social assistance loans for emergencies and pay advances. Enjoying the same benefit, workers shared a common identity; they all possessed the same rights, rights that the company was legally obligated to uphold.

The extension of equal rights helped workers to come together and put aside regional ties. As one worker recalled, "It no longer mattered what province you were from but whether or not you were in the union." The talareño argolla quickly broke up as many of its members affiliated with the new organization. In the same way, those who became union leaders were united by bonds of fraternity and cooperation rooted in a common will to promote the organization. The group that started the union was composed of workers who came from diverse places: two from Ayacucho, two from Lima (one from the city and another from Cajatambo), two from Piura, one from Chiclayo, one from Cajamarca, and one from Apurímac. Workers from this initial group held seats on the General Secretaría (governing board) of the union during the first seven years. The workers who succeeded them were also from different parts of the country: Ancash, Cajamarca, Piura, and Callao. A new sense of solidarity among all workers displaced the old feelings of solidarity based on regional background. This sense was expressed in different ways. Some of the clasista talareños refused to take it personally when someone would make reference to those "shithead talareños." Clasista union leaders coined an expression that modified the insult to avoid conflicts with the compañeros talareños. They decided that there were two kinds of talareños: plain talareños and "shithead talareños." The differences and frictions between criollos and serranos dissipated in time because of the union organization and the way it transformed workers' attitudes. As one worker put it: "We were no longer what we used to be before. There was none of that he earns more because he's a criollo or that because he's from the interior he makes less." The union organization brought people together as equals. It was now of crucial importance that workers stand united to demand benefits, resist speed-ups in production on the factory floor, and in the last instance, strike. From the perspective of a serrano worker, "the criollos were understanding that no matter how brave or criollo they might be, by being alone they would definitely be isolated." A criollo worker observed:

> When we set up the union, we set aside these fights and personal beefs with the serranos on behalf of working together so they [the abuses] would be eliminated. The serranos were taught that they also had to think about the list of demands. Then, we said to them, look, we're all in a struggle to look for a way to get one more sol for the benefit of all of us. You're fucking up and carrying stuff all the time and you go on busting ass and we're over here trying to come up with what to do so that we might all together make a couple more soles too. You're screwing up and you don't care about anything and you're very happy with your wage. Then the cholo got educated and changed his tune.

The management's view on the homogenization of the workforce was described by an executive: "The difference between criollos and serranos is that the latter are hard to understand when they talk and have a hard time understanding when spoken to. It takes them a while to understand. A criollo, after a few years, wants to become a lathe operator and an Andean worker doesn't. But other than that, once they make demands on the employer, they are all just the same."

3

Fighting for Benefits
The Limits of the Clasista Union

The Metal Empresa union was organized and led by a group of workers known as clasistas. These clasista leaders believed that workers would win concessions from the company only if they engaged in what they referred to as la lucha—a militant struggle.

La lucha was a concept with clear political connotations. Clasista union leaders identified with Peru's New Left. The New Left, with its origins in universities, viewed itself as the *vanguardia consciente* (conscious vanguard) of the working class. The Left sought to mobilize the working class in opposition to what it identified as the "bourgeois reformist" military governments of the 1970s. An important segment of the Left had been shaped by the political thought of Ernesto "Che" Guevara, the hero of the Cuban Revolution. Guevara's ideas about creating a *foco* (nucleus) of political and military action in the form of a guerrilla organization were especially influential in thinking on the Left. The foco model was something that the Left sought to replicate in the course of organizing the working class. According to vanguardia logic, the goal of the party was to gain control over union leaders and their organizations in order to promote and lead the workers' struggle. The clasista leaders routinely analyzed the situation in factories at party meetings. On the basis of these discussions, according to former union leader Jesús Zúñiga, the party decided "what points to raise so that the workers might be mobilized."

For clasista leaders, la lucha was not just a way of extracting concessions from the company. It was important in and of itself, maybe more than any benefits gained per se. One member of the workers' groups involved in assessing whether or not strike conditions existed in the factory described the evaluation process. According to him, the evaluation included "two dimensions: (1) the response of the masses, if it was combative or not, if it was weakened in some way or not; and (2) the extent to which demands had been met on previous occasions." As the worker put it, "Reducing the evaluation [of the strike] to only the second aspect is to fall into simple-minded economism."[1] The workers' struggle as such constituted the principal justification for the union leaders to exercise the functions given to them by the clasista workers.

At the same time, in the face of the company's despotic and discriminatory treatment, la lucha proved to be an effective strategy to obtain benefits. From the beginning, workers acknowledged the effectiveness of the strategy proposed by the clasistas. Workers were convinced that to guarantee any improvement in benefits, it was not enough for the union just to present a proposal and negotiate with the company. They knew they had to be willing to strike if necessary. Workers had great expectations when the union presented its first list of demands to the company. Because of the surplus in the labor market, the company did not offer anything in response to the union proposal for a wage hike. That provoked a strike that lasted fourteen days. When the Ministry of Labor resolved the dispute by mandating an increase of fifteen soles, workers were disappointed. "At the assembly a lot of people wept," Jesús Zúñiga related, "and they agreed to strike for one more day for free, just to make a point. Far from being frightened by that strike, people went back to work feeling strengthened. Everyone was aware that, thanks to that type of struggle, they had won a victory of fifteen soles when the company wouldn't offer us absolutely anything."

The workers' belief in the effectiveness of the strike as a bargaining tool was confirmed by the company's behavior. Workers discovered that their right to articulate grievances and request improvements, albeit recognized by the company, was much more apparent than real. The union would draw up its demands and the company would sit down to talk about them, but that did not mean than any meaningful negotiation was taking place. The company resisted incorporating the demands of workers in policies as a product of negotiations with the union. "The company acted like it didn't have anything and that it couldn't concede," Jesús Zúñiga said. Workers were denied access to data about the company's financial status. Information about the company's finances would have provided the basis for a real negotiation with the company. The union attempted to get around this difficulty by making use of the legal procedures provided for in the Industrial Community Law; once they contracted accountants to conduct a study of the company's finances. The official financial accounts, however, indicated that the company was nearly broke.

Workers found that hard to believe because of the volume of production they saw at the plant. As one worker recalled, "Everybody there thought there was fraud, but there was no way to prove it." The lack of reliable information about the company's finances caused enormous distrust among workers, especially when they compared the official information with what they knew about what was going on in the factory. Percy Hinojosa observed:

> The factory never shows any profits. During the fifteen years it has been in operation, it didn't make a profit a single year even though it has had plenty of work orders. Why does it go on working if it loses? I think the company isn't losing money. It always earns a profit and we think that they must have one set of books for them and another for us. Many times in industrial community meetings, the managers stated that there was a lot of work and that this time they're definitely going to make a profit, at least some. But at the end of the year the company still posted losses. It did not earn anything at all and is indebted. This is because, according to them, they took out a loan to stay in business. I think it must be a maneuver by the company.

This lack of confidence in the company naturally intensified the workers' faith in their union organization, laying the groundwork for strike activity.

At the same time, workers found that the government—the entity that was supposed to guarantee collective bargaining and that controlled the final outcome of negotiations through its power to set wage increases—was an unreliable institutional actor. Workers went on learning negative lessons. They learned not to expect the protection of state institutions. They learned not to have confidence in the business's bookkeeping records. They learned not to believe in the company's rhetoric about its will to negotiate. They learned not to rely on the alleged impartiality of the state bureaucracy in its role as mediator. Luis Pretell summarized the problem:

> The workers have absolutely nothing to protect them. The constitution, the law, says the Ministry of Labor exercises an overseer's function of guardianship over workers but none of that power is exercised in favor of the working class. It's just the opposite. The ministry defends the employer, or entrepreneur. Workers surely know how

much they have worked and how much they have produced during the year. They don't have statistics about all the issues but they know—in the case of a shipyard worker—how many ships have been built and they more or less know how much it costs to put this boat on the market, how much has been invested in sheet metal planks, in welding, in manual labor, and how much he's going to earn. But there's no mechanism for making the case, nor any documentary proof to offer the Ministry of Labor. It's his [the worker's] word against the employer's balance sheets and even if he might have enough proof, they say it's fraudulent and illegal. Therefore, all of this needs to be changed, to look for another way so that the Labor Ministry might work for change that really is in line with the constitution. Here they talk a lot about how we're democratic and that we defend human rights. But that's all on paper, just theory. Because in practice, if they don't kill us with bullets, they starve us and it's just that—even the newspapers say it—the reasons for that subversive movement [Sendero Luminoso] are apparent. Many people say, if they're going to kill me kneeling, it's better then to be killed standing up. Therefore, if you really want change, the best thing to do is to cut this evil out at the root, this blight which calls itself the Ministry of Labor.

In short, given the refusal of the company to recognize workers as legitimate actors as well as the failure of the state to act as an honest broker in negotiations, workers learned to trust the strike. It was the only way to fight for benefits despite the risks and costs it entailed. "When you think about going out on strike," Luis Pretell explained, "we know that we're going to lose some income and that there is an economic downside for our families. But the strike is necessary because if we don't go on strike we'll always be on our knees, with less income, at the employer's mercy." As another worker, Pedro Aquije, commented, "You get things by fighting and any other way you don't get anything." For that reason, the clasista union, more than just being an organization set up to make demands and bargain, was a *fighting* machine designed to *protest and pressure*. With demand making as its raison d'être and la lucha as its modus operandi, the union was an organized response to the arbitrary and discriminatory practices that workers had endured.

Thus la lucha became the link that united leaders willing to represent workers (if, by doing so, radical political mobilization could be achieved), with workers ready to engage in radical activity (if, through that, they would obtain benefits). In other words, clasistas, with the help of the party, aided workers by providing the leadership that unions needed to press their demands successfully. In exchange, workers provided a valued political resource for the Left in the context of a dictatorial government—namely, their mobilization.

Between the union leaders and the workers, a leader-follower relationship was established in which workers delegated responsibility to leaders for the management of la lucha. In return, workers showed a willingness to mobilize in order to support the actions of their leaders whenever they were called together for that purpose. On their part, leaders were ready to take on those responsibilities in exchange for the power to mobilize workers.

Workers delegated union leaders the power to decide when they should or should not act. The power and moral authority enjoyed by union leaders was recognized; it overshadowed the democratic formalities associated with the internal governance of the union. One worker put it this way:

> What people like to have is a boss who leads them, who decides their fate. If Quiroz said something stopped here, it stopped. Nobody refuted his judgment. The problems in the handling of the list of demands were taken practically as a formality to the assembly. There was, for example, an assembly in 1976, where the battle about the list of demands was being discussed. Several compañeros got up and said that it was necessary to take the company's offer. There was a compañero who got up and said, "Speaking as a red-blooded male and the family man that I am, as far as I'm concerned, let's go with it [the company's offer]." A total of ten guys had spoken when Delmer Quiroz got up and gave a convincing talk in support of the strike. When he got through, the assembly approved the strike, and thanks to that, the company gave us two more soles.

Workers sought to elect as union leader someone who was seen as a proactive fighter. A leader had to be brave and bold. In other words, he had to be someone able to put up with dangerous and conflictual situations. The workers' principal leader, Delmer Quiroz, became famous in the factory even before he was a leader for having risked his life by putting out a fire in a bottle of acetylene. Because being a union leader involved taking greater risks (i.e., exposing oneself to employers' reprisals and perhaps even dismissal), leadership positions were assumed mainly by those who had less to lose, namely younger workers. What usually distinguished clasista leaders was not that they came from the same region or had the same skill or section assignment in the factory. Their common trait — attacked scornfully and mocked by the older, more conciliatory workers — was their youth.

For the rank-and-file worker, the union was not simply an organization for deliberation and participation in the collective bargaining process. To a worker, the union was a group made up of leaders who played in a game on his behalf and called the shots as to how it would be conducted. Union leaders were there to decide what radical actions would be used to extract concessions from the company. In addition, union leaders were there to defend and protect the worker from the company. In other words, the pact between the leaders and the rank and file was not just that between leader and follower, it was *paternalistic* as well. The rank-and-file worker gave his support to the union leader, who took charge of defending and protecting him in his dealings with the company. Given the problems that he had experienced in the company, Percy Hinojosa joined the union looking for security. As he put it, in order "to see who might defend me, as I was thinking about that, I joined the union." In exchange for that security and protection, the worker was willing to follow his leader. The principal union leader, Delmer Quiroz, recognized this:

> What you said about the workers' readiness to delegate practically all their interests and perogatives to the persons who led them was a tendency. Indeed, if somebody does a study about the social and cultural reality of our country, one would have to recognize that there's a subservient attitude. Unfortunately, this is a country with people who have backbones of jelly because we have been oppressed. Accustomed as we are to have someone crushing us underfoot, with our heads bowed low, for so many centuries, okay, it's just natural that if somebody says to you, look buddy, I'm going to defend you, you feel like saying, "Thanks, man." That's normal.[2]

The establishment of the union put an end to the old relations of dependency in the factory. But it did not eliminate the workers' need to depend on someone for protection. In exchange for that protection, workers were willing to delegate responsibility for the decisions that union leaders made on their behalf. Workers respectfully recognized the personal qualities of those who showed an ability to relate to company officials. The *leader* had to be somebody who knew how to *speak* or, as the workers said, someone who knew how "to get in their two cents' worth." This was extremely important to workers because the company "didn't pay attention to us, didn't attach any importance to us," Esteban Vilcahuamán recalled. "[We'd be] like a person to whom nobody would listen and we [the leaders] had to speak [for them]." The union leader had to be able to handle the language of characters as different as the Andean migrant, the Labor Ministry bureaucrat, the personnel manager, and also, of course, the party official. The leader was effectively a kind of social polyglot. This communicative role was handled best by those who had more education and more experience in the city. The union leaders, even if they were of provincial origin, had come as children to the city after having been enrolled in school for several years. Moreover, union leaders generally had relatively advanced educational credentials. Delmer Quiroz stood out in this regard. Along with having finished high school, he had studied on his own so that he had a background equal to that of any good university student.

The leader personally took it upon himself to protect each rank-and-file worker and defend him. As many leaders admitted, that defense took place even "if he [the worker] might not be right." The leaders made a major case out of every incident identified by the workers as an expression of mistreatment. Whenever such a situation came up, the leader intervened in defense of the worker. For example, if it was a matter of a warning to a worker, the union leader would immediately demand that a meeting be held between the supervisor and the worker, with himself and the personnel manager also present. This practice invested the union leader with a certain amount of authority to judge what had happened at the lower levels of the company hierarchy. At times, the union even managed to reverse the punishments meted out by the company. It did so by publicly criticizing the company's actions in the union newspaper. Because of its wide circulation among factories on Avenida Argentina, the union newspaper was feared by employers for its ability to disseminate negative publicity. In this way, leaders rendered inoperative the suspensions handed down against the workers. But in addition, on one occasion, leaders threatened a work stoppage to protest what had been a just suspension levied on a worker who had been found asleep on the job. "We knew the company was right," a former leader admitted, "but as a matter of principle, it was necessary to defend the worker."

All of this altered the authority relations inside the factory in ways that controlled abuses and clarified the lines of authority. "When we set up the union," Esteban Vilcahuamán related, "we were completely changed; I mean, quite clearly, we had all kept our heads bowed before, but when we started our union, we all held our heads up; [the union] was an enormous defense for us. There were no longer any abuses or countermands. Before the manager would come, he'd give an order, then the engineer would come, he'd issue an order, the supervisor would come, he'd give an order, a clerk would come, he'd order something, so that everybody was giving orders. Then from the moment when we set up the union, we cut out that line. Here we only pay attention to the supervisor and nobody else."

To a certain extent, a situation was created in which, as one leader in a union assembly declared, "The workers impose the discipline." The idea of workers controlling what happened on the factory floor was unwelcome by management. A company official observed, "First, there was despotic treatment from the company and later the despotic treatment came from the union. Deep down, both are bad. But the tyrannical treatment of the company is creative, while the tyrannical treatment of the union is destructive." The change in the internal structure of authority relationships created an atmosphere that some workers took advantage of to slow down on the job.

The policy of worker protection also included social welfare. For the most part, it was handled directly by the union itself through the Secretaría de Asistencia Social (Secretariat of Social Welfare). The secretaría, which was considered "the most important" part of the union by some leaders, was in charge of offering support to workers in exceptional cases of need—illness, the birth of a child, and death of close relatives. It was a cooperative system that depended on the support of the workers, whether it be through monetary contributions, blood donations, or other kinds of mutual aid. For workers, "union" signified a safe haven. It was an invaluable source of support in the midst of the ups and downs of city life.

The top union bosses reinforced the dependence of workers on the leaders in a variety of ways. The leader, for example, would act as the intermediary between the worker and the company for obtaining loans and other benefits. On the other hand, the vast majority of unskilled workers, mainly youths and migrants, were protected by the leaders in personnel classification procedures. Union leaders opposed job classification examinations for unskilled workers because they believed that most would fail. Instead, they proposed a pay raise scheme that brought unskilled workers closer to the pay levels of most skilled workers. This policy, incidentally, made the most qualified and experienced workers resentful and alienated them from the union.

By providing important services, the leader gained the support and *confianza* (trust) of the rank-and-file worker. "I used to feel the total confidence of the majority of the compañeros," Delmer Quiroz remembered. "I was even a sex counselor [to them], people could trust me." Union leaders took advantage of the power delegated to them to exclude those who disagreed with them and impose their own union and political line. Dissenting voices were not tolerated. As a former leader recognized, "Here you couldn't object, the person who objected was left out." The union forbade the distribution of newspapers from opposing political groups. Rank-and-file workers did not dare express disagreement with their leaders.

After six years of clasista leadership, the growing estrangement between clasista leaders and workers was never discussed openly by the workers. In other words, workers would accept the proposals of the clasistas in the assembly, but then they would do just the opposite. That is what happened in regard to the "question of principles" posed by the union in 1976. Union leaders took the position that it would be unacceptable for the company to be allowed to default on its obligation to give a leather jacket to each worker by paying a sum of money equal in value to the jacket. The jacket deal was stipulated in the collective contract, but the jackets were unavailable on the market. In this case, after having approved the proposal to reject the monetary settlement in the assembly, the workers proceeded to collect the money offered by the company. Their behavior obliged union leaders to change their stance. The same thing happened when workers began to object to the union leaders' opposition to a policy of economic incentives proposed by the company. Union leaders opposed the policy on the justifiable fear that it would undermine, as it eventually did, the internal cohesion of the union. The incentives policy established the idea that economic gains could be had outside of the union.

The union was organized around two different kinds of relationships. In its relations with the company, the union insisted on the principles of due process and equality in the treatment of the workers. At the same time, inside the union, relations of personal dependence were reproduced. For a majority of workers, the relationship with the union was hierarchical and paternalistic. For the minority that opposed the union, the relationship was authoritarian and exclusionary.

In the philosophy of relations espoused by clasistas, the clasista leader was an intermediary between the political group that supported him as a leader in order to mobilize workers and those mobilized workers who were compensated by the union's success in obtaining benefits. Through the clasista leaders and their connection to the rank and file, leftist groups established a clientele network that could be used for political mobilization against the military government.[3]

As time passed, difficulties emerged in the relationships among workers, union leaders, and leftist activists. Clasista union leaders came face-to-face with a new set of demands from skilled workers. The demands emerged in response to important technical changes that were taking place in the factory. These changes fortified a sense of professionalism among skilled workers. After the establishment of the union, the company's earnings no longer could be based on maintaining depressed wages or on despotic control over time on the job. Those policies were no longer an option because workers had discovered the strike as a mechanism they could wield to pressure the company for raises and to curb mistreatment. It became apparent that the profitability of the company could be maintained and increased only by taking the path that the company adopted in 1972: introducing technical innovations to increase productivity. Because of the characteristics of the metallurgical industry, technical innovation was not simply a question of mechanizing the production process to increase productivity. Rather, modernization of the plant meant that workers needed to become more qualified, with improved job skills.

To accomplish this goal, the company contracted a group of Japanese technicians from the Ishika-Wayima Corporation who taught new techniques to company personnel. The Japanese, for example, taught a new welding technique that involved holding the pliers upward when welding instead of using the conventional method of holding the pliers downward. This upward technique made it possible to weld from a variety of positions. It made welding faster and increased productivity. They also taught a technique that sped up the bending of sheet metal by applying heat in set points of the sheet. One worker described the new method: "Before, all the bending was done by brute force. In contrast, when the sheet was heated up, it would bend by itself and give way like a piece of paper. Now working on iron for us is like grabbing a sheet of paper but before it wasn't, before we'd do it by brute strength so we were pulling one thing or another." The Japanese also taught other techniques such as putting ships together by sections.

All of these changes created new tensions and conflicts that had nothing to do with the argolla or regional differences between workers. New demands from the highly skilled workers were expressed in conflicts between sections and trades. They complained that there was, in a manner of speaking, excessive equality. "It was thought," said one worker, "that if one worker had to have lunch at one time, another would too, and if one had earned more, so did the other also." From the onset, opposition to the leadership took hold in the section from the Maestranza, a section made up of workers who had precision jobs and were highly skilled. The plant lathe operators, for example, were in this section.

There were sections in the factory that were organized as workshops, such as the operations that built boilers and machines and the sections or teams that worked outside building the ships. The skilled workers from these workshops played up their differences with other plant workers. They considered themselves shop workers and scorned other workers to whom they referred as being from *la pampa* (i.e., outside). They bragged that "not anybody just gets into the shops." But when there was a union assembly, the great majority of workers were from la pampa, not the workshops. They won the votes, rejecting the repeated proposals of the skilled workers that workers be evaluated in reference to educational credentials and experience. One labor leader rebutted the argument made by skilled workers that they were special cases: "Here we all are special cases, we're all family men." But resentment was felt even among the original founders of the union and led some skilled workers to split from the union.

Later in 1975, the more skilled workers from la pampa who worked in the boat welding section put forth their own proposal. They demanded a wage increase on the basis of their advanced skills as welders. The entire section supported this claim. The group was led by a worker from the original clasistas. The union was opposed to giving them special treatment and negotiated a special raise for everybody. But after this conflict, a new discussion about differences arose in the factory. This time it was between welders and boilermakers, with each one demanding better pay and status. The welder demanded that he "ought to be better paid than the boilermaker because on his job you had to work in a certain posture, and besides outside technicians would be coming to see if his work was done well by using x-rays to see if it had leaks or internal cracks. If a rivet isn't done right, the welding pops open and it is there you can see the welder's experience. On the other hand, the job of the boilermaker is to execute a blueprint and nothing else." The boilermaker in turn protested that he should be "classified at a top rank because to be a boilermaker, you have to have as a minimum a grade school education. The welding trade doesn't require much preparation because welding is a matter of hands-on training and nothing more."

Workers chose to collect the money offered by the company in lieu of the leather jackets, thereby violating a union agreement. That same year, the workers overwhelmingly accepted the system of individual production incentives proposed by the company despite the opposition of the governing board of the union. The regimen of incentives provided economic benefits to individual workers based on their performance. The system undermined the union. The new incentives weakened the importance of the union organization among the workers by undermining the importance of the union leaders and diminishing their capacity to mobilize workers to participate in work stoppages and strikes. But as one labor leader reflected, "In fact our opposition was mainly centered on the ideological content of an incentives policy which, as we have already come to appreciate in practice, tends to break down the levels of class consciousness that the workers may have been able to absorb. The clearest example of this problem was the disapproval by the rank and file of the General Strike of 1976 called by the Federación de Trabajadores de la Industria Metalúrgica del Perú (FETIMP)."[4]

In 1976, the company used the incentives program to speed up production on a ship contract. Workers earned additional pay according to how well they succeeded in reducing the time necessary to finish their jobs. This stimulated a notable increase in the work pace and also in the availability of overtime for workers. In exchange, they earned exceptionally high wages. The economic windfall allowed many workers to build additions to their homes and make other major expenditures.

As several contracts neared completion in 1977, the company's production declined. The company planned a downsizing of personnel by offering a retirement package to the workers. Once again, many workers preferred to select the company's option rather than take the clasista position in defense of their jobs which their leaders might have preferred. Of a total of 420 workers, 180 accepted the company's proposal between August and November 1976. Instead of heading a "struggle against downsizing," as had been their intention, leaders instead had to take charge of negotiating a larger sum in severance pay to encourage retirements at the request of the workers.

With their judgment clouded by the trust that they had enjoyed in the past — thinking that workers solidly supported the ideology they advocated — clasista leaders were not willing to accept that workers might want to pursue their individual interests outside of the framework provided by the union or even abandon being factory workers altogether. Disappointed by the realization that workers did not want to remain proletarians, some clasista workers themselves left the company for independent activities. Others stayed but brooded over the fact that workers did not stand by clasismo as they had hoped. Those who remained as leaders noticed the changes in workers' attitudes. "At the time of the incentives," Freddy Llamocca related, "the leaders ended up by themselves, the work stoppages and strikes were not like before. The people were getting bored with the job actions, with the strikes. The leaders called them to assemblies for work stoppages and they no longer wanted to go." After calling an assembly, the former leader Villón recalled, "some people even said that we did it just to screw around."

Instead of recognizing the causes underlying the changes in workers' attitudes, the union leaders chose to blame themselves for the estrangement. A few comments indicate how union leaders processed the events: "Through self-criticism, we must identify how our political weakness led us to faults like the ones pointed out, having neglected our job of clarification and greater consciousness raising of the rank and file. This weakness did not allow us to correctly pose the ideological meaning of the incentives to the mass of workers." Since it was easier for the leaders to feel guilty than to find out what the real political leanings of the workers were, the clasista group proposed to "reinforce the political work in the leaders group, to propagandize to the maximum the central points of the current report, combat indiscipline, [and] to participate more actively with other clasista forces, whether at the level of the metallurgical federation or in general."[5]

From then on, clasistas used the demands of the workers as a pretext to mobilize workers to participate in work stoppages and strikes. Union leaders considered such actions increasingly important as the authoritarianism of the military government became more pronounced. One union leader, Daniel Angulo, described the logic:

> On one occasion, the company owed us thirteen lunch pails. During the school year, whoever had more than three children got a lunch pail from the company. But the company didn't comply and always said it was going to give us one next week. So we decided that either they'd give us the lunch pails or we were going to have a work stoppage in protest. This was in 1977. We had a protest work stoppage on behalf of the thirteen lunch pails. We missed a day and a Sunday pay. I understand that when you do a protest work stoppage, it's to win and not to lose. So with thirteen lost shifts we would have had enough to pay for twenty-six lunchboxes. Who won? Us or the company? If we look at it on one side, it's okay, we set a precedent that the company ought to comply in accordance with the collective contract. But you also have to look on the economic side. You're throwing away a day and Sunday's pay from a family man. There were some people who didn't have more than a single child. Out of eight hundred persons, for thirteen lunch pails, are you going to throw away a day's pay and Sunday pay in a work stoppage?

Workers' demands were also used as an excuse to gain their participation in marches and solidarity work stoppages. A worker from the clasista nucleus recalled,

> Sometimes when a march for the CGTP would be proposed, the people didn't want to go and since we were in the leadership, we'd manipulate or, that is, we'd force them to do it. We knew how to appeal to the masses in such a way that they'd go and we'd convince them that they had to go. It was a question of leadership ability. Some would say to us: you're steamrolling us. We'd argue that we couldn't allow the company's abuse to go on because there were some agreements which weren't being kept or other problems with the company. We'd say, if we don't let the public know about our problems, the

company isn't going to resolve them. If the public finds out, the customers are going to find out and that's important, compañeros.

But once workers were at the demonstration, they would chant political slogans as well as union ones.

The clasistas lobbied workers to support the FETIMP strike of 5–6 September 1978. A union leader brought a group of miners, on whose behalf the work action had been called, to the factory doors. The Metal Empresa workers subsequently supported the work stoppage but not without grumbling.

The fragmentation of the Left and the competition among different groups to take over unions and use them to lead the political opposition to the government only served to alienate workers more. Workers did not see any way in which the ideological disputes and power struggles within the Left were related to a better defense of their interests. The disarray of the political groups also affected the Metal Empresa union, and the union leaders began to compete among themselves. As the former leader Feliciano Pacheco recognized, "There were disagreements over political leanings and each one wanted to have control of the union." The disputes arose on ideological grounds that were incomprehensible to the average worker. As union leader Daniel Angulo observed, "Some said that what José Carlos Mariátegui meant was this and others said it wasn't, that what Mariátegui meant with those words was something else and then from that, the fight would start."[6] For the average worker otherwise identified with the clasistas, these arguments were the vehicles through which different groups would "attack each other. The first thing that they tried to do was to make their compañero look bad." The fact that such discrepancies arose made workers feel dubious and further alienated them from their leaders. "Why did they disagree?" Angulo wondered. "If there was an agreement on ideas, then why would Calvo disagree with Pacheco? For years, they had the same opinions. What did people think then? No, they say, there's something here, a dirty trick; they must be fighting among themselves for something."

The biggest problem, however, was not the confusion the leaders' ideological disputes created for the workers but that the conflicts had consequences for the life of the union itself. The purpose of these discussions was not, in the first instance, ideological clarification. Rather, they were part of the competition to capture the union leadership. In the conflict, competing groups were ready to place their political objectives first even when that might harm the rank and file. One internal document of the group Trinchera Roja characterized the situation as follows:

> Once the political organization which had responsibility for leading the union was split up, this breakup was reflected in the division of the former board of directors. From then on a struggle arose between two wings for hegemony in the union. This is natural and will continue to go on in the future. The NEGATIVE PART, and that's what we ought to criticize here, is the way in which the fight has gone on in a way that is detrimental to the union's united front. We're saying this because, at various points in time, the compañeros who are aligned with VR [Vanguardia Revolucionaria] have fallen into sectarianism, hegemonic intents, and in putting their interests ahead of those of the masses [by sabotaging the work of the new leadership].[7]

The document went on to point out, "When the ex-press secretary tried to prevent compañeros from the other wing from participating with articles in *Labor* [the union newspaper], that went beyond the understanding of the rank and file, confusing it and adding fuel to the fire of the reactionaries."

Between 1976 and 1979 the misunderstandings between clasista leaders and workers accumulated and increasingly distanced one from the other. The clasistas felt more and more disappointed. Under these conditions, it no longer seemed reasonable to some clasistas to make the enormous sacrifices associated with assuming leadership positions, such as missing the opportunity for overtime pay, spending free time on union business, and handling conflicts with the company that could entail the risk of being fired. In exchange for the sacrifices and the benefits they got for the workers, union leaders expected workers to abide by their views on politics and trade unionism. In the absence of such a relationship, union leaders also began to think of ways to quit. In 1976, overwhelmed by the weight of his responsibilities to his fellow workers, Delmer Quiroz decided to give up not only his powers as a union leader but his factory job too. The entire group of renowned leaders who had begun clasista unionism in the company followed him. Celestino Peralta, Jesús Zúñiga, and Feliciano Pacheco went into partnership to set up a metallurgical shop on Avenida Argentina, a few blocks away from the factory. They named the place the "Olympic." Feliciano Pacheco considered that his possibilities for promotion in the factory were limited by the fact he had been a union leader:

> I saw that there wouldn't be a future for me and I had gotten married a little before and had to think of myself. By then, they [fellow workers] had spoken to me about setting up a small business to work for ourselves. We had worked in the company and had got the monster moving, don't you think now we ought to do it for ourselves? A compañero spoke to me and said okay, we've been holding ourselves back for eight years now on behalf of other compañeros and we haven't even had the opportunity to take care of our own family and home. I think it's about time we thought about ourselves. Here in the company, you only get the company's hate. We practically don't have a future. Tomorrow or the next day, they'll kick you out or you leave—you end up the same.

Their many years of experience in the factory gave the leaders an added advantage. Their participation in the organization and management of the union gave leaders the know-how and confidence to set up their own workshop. "It seemed that the history of setting up the union was repeating itself," Feliciano Pacheco recalled, "when Quiroz decided to form the union through a directive from the political party. Then he said, if we had the ability to organize the union and manage it, then I think we have as much capacity to set up a small shop and work." At that point, Jesús Zúñiga decided to quit and join the group forming an independent workshop. "At the start," he related, "we were a single fist, united against the employers. Whatever the [union] leader proposed was achieved. The other side of the coin is that after having spoiled the people from Metal Empresa—in other words, they got everything due to a strong union—the workers neither supported nor defended the persons fired in 1977. I had to defend myself. So I quit and went to the assembly and like a man, I said: I quit. Any questions? And nobody said anything."

The clasista leaders who stayed felt disillusioned with their fellow workers. One of the remaining leaders noted that the people "didn't have political consciousness. The people are like a tide, they go out with the one who gives them something." The workers, in turn, reproached the leaders for having pressured them and pushed for mobilizations and strikes using their demands as a pretext. "They took us to the marches," Rolando Luzquiño said. "Once they subjected us to a march for I don't know what party," another worker complained, "but we went on the condition of publicizing our struggle. We didn't get involved to support their politics. Our goal was to get benefits for our families." While reticent about openly rejecting the pressures from the clasistas, the majority of workers were becoming resentful of leaders. A rank-and-file worker expressed this resentment in the assembly that followed the forced strike of the Federación Metalúrgica in September 1978 when he said that the clasistas "were always deceitful." Starting in 1980, workers did not elect the clasistas again but looked to a different group for leadership. This group was made up of some of the best-known spokesmen for the demands of the skilled workers. They included Ramón Espinoza and Bartolomé Valverde, who for years had felt alienated from the union.

The intense trust that existed between workers and leaders had been the basis of a relationship that contributed simultaneously to the success and the weakness of the union. The rapid ascent of clasistas to positions was due to their ability to function in a relationship in which they repaid workers' support with effective protection and their leadership in la lucha. The relationship worked successfully as long as the union was a channel for improving the lot of the workers. Once circumstances changed as a result of the overall change in the conditions affecting the industry and opportunities that reduced the importance of unions, workers pragmatically opted for change. They prepared themselves to cast aside not only the union but even their own status as wage earners. Once the possibility of obtaining benefits through union actions lost importance, workers were not disposed to follow the orders of their union leaders. At the same time, union leaders could not come to terms with the fact that the rank and file lacked a strong class consciousness. The disenchantment between leaders and followers was mutual; the link that had united clasista leaders and workers was broken. In other words, the idea that improvements would be won by uniting workers in the union's struggle was dead. Workers no longer saw any sense in keeping union activity to a maximum. They stopped feeling that they ought to continue supporting other unions. They did not even defend their own leaders when they were fired. Once clasismo trade unions ceased to be viewed as effective, workers did not feel inclined to live up to the obligations that their pact with the leaders had involved. Once the pact was broken, the relationship itself broke up.

The loyalties among workers, clasista leaders, and leftist parties were based on the effectiveness of relationships that were pragmatic, instrumental, and reciprocal. The relationships and the loyalties turned out to be precarious. The different players, in the midst of fluid and changing situations, made cost-benefit calculations and shifted their alliances. The workers of Metal Empresa reassessed the appropriateness of following the orders of the clasistas and keeping them on as leaders. The leaders, for their part, concluded that if they could not get workers to go along with their initiatives, it was not worthwhile to assume the personal costs of leadership. After a few months, union leaders gave up the cause of unionism to take on the new risk of being small-scale entrepreneurs. The political parties that organized the workers' movement in the 1970s also reassessed the utility of continuing to use unions as their core political base and questioned whether they should move on to other, more promising venues.

Then, as now, social loyalties based on reciprocity were precarious in Peru. There is a basic mistrust that characterizes Peruvian society. A permanent sense of mistrust always lies underneath the occasional expressions of trust that take place. The most experienced clasista leaders were apt to recommend, for example, that workers maintain an attitude of distrust toward their own leaders. The advice was a precaution against the eventuality of a shift in alliances by leaders (for example, if union leaders decided to ally themselves with the company and negotiate the workers' demands for their own benefit). Therefore, according to Jaime Cáceres from the Federación Metalúrgica, "it's natural that there's distrust." Not only that: "It seems to me that it's right that it exists and that we can't oblige workers to blindly believe in their leaders. That would be bad. That creates caudillos and false idols."

4

Acting Like Workers

In the 1970s, metallurgical unions shared a commitment to la lucha—the militant struggle that won tangible material gains for rank-and-file workers. The unions supported the various work stoppages, strikes, and mobilizations called for by the Federación Metalúrgica, the umbrella organization for the clasista unions in the metallurgical industry. From 1970 to 1975, membership in the Federación increased from 15 to 115 company unions.[1] On a bigger scale, the Federación replicated the caudillismo that was typical of clasista unions. It acted as a central command, directing the actions that unions took in the course of la lucha.

Unions were ordered to mobilize for purposes other than that of extracting specific concessions from their own companies. Sometimes, the Federación called on unions to act in solidarity with other unions involved in labor disputes; sometimes unions were called together by the Federación to make demands on the state to ensure that their rights were respected. The Federación, however, did not provide services to its affiliated unions. Each union managed its own relationship with its respective company. But the Federación empowered individual unions by increasing their ability to pressure employers and protect themselves from reprisals by the state. The Federación was not a staid institution that presided over a stable union movement. Rather, it was an organization for taking action.

Among themselves, unions established relations of reciprocity to facilitate la lucha. Namely, they supported each other's actions and allied with each other to defend themselves vis-à-vis the state. To these ends, they turned to the most valuable resource they had: their capacity to mobilize and strike.

Preexisting practices of mutual support among unions at the neighborhood level laid the basis for broad-based reciprocity among the metallurgical unions. During their first strike, workers from Metal Empresa received material and moral support from unions in their neighborhood, mainly the metallurgical ones. That established a sense of obligation among the workers of Metal Empresa to support their fellow workers in similar circumstances. Feliciano Pacheco recalled, "When we called our first strike without experience of any kind, several unions came out to give us encouragement and economic support." On different occasions, workers would make donations to support other unions in conflict. Union leaders acted as consultants to other unions in the industrial zone of Avenida Argentina, offering constant guidance and support on how to build the infrastructure of a union and develop its activities. Thus workers extrapolated from their own union experience and extended the concept of mutual support beyond the walls of their own factory.

Solidarity among workers from the same industrial sector was common. Metallurgical workers recognized that they shared similar conditions and problems. Among the metallurgical unions, mutual support was practiced among unions from the same neighborhood. Workers contributed to strike funds and participated in marches, work stoppages, and strikes in support of all the unions in conflict. As seen in Table 2, mutual support was an outstanding feature in the way metallurgical unions conducted themselves between 1972 and 1979.

The commitment to mutual support through radical collective action manifested itself in the first strike called by metallurgical unions in June 1972. That commitment was evident in all the subsequent work stoppages and strikes of the 1970s. In their demands, the unions always included a request for a resolution of the labor conflicts involving metallurgical unions and the rehiring of fired workers. Metallurgical unions reached out even to workers from other regions of the country in expressions of solidarity. From 1972 on, the metallurgical workers went on strike to reject governmental intervention in and repression of mineworkers' unions, iron and steelworkers' unions, and fishermen's unions. At the same time, the metallurgical unions supported fired and indicted union leaders in different sectors of industry and rejected the layoffs of workers from other industrial branches such as plastics and footwear. In these cases, the expression of solidarity overlapped with the defense of the principle that the government should not interfere with unions. That principle was deemed to be in the interest of all unionized workers. But in addition to this participation, workers even mobilized in support of the people of another country: there were marches in support of the Chilean people (and the Allende government) in November 1972 and September 1973.

TABLE 2. *Work Stoppages, Marches, and Strikes by Metallurgical Unions, 1972–1977*

Year	Event	Stated Objectives
June 1972	24-hour work stoppage	In support of unions on strike, against subcontracting companies, for job security, for working-class political autonomy, to abolish biannual claims negotiation
3 November 1972	March	To publicize the 48-hour work stoppage, in solidarity with the Chilean people
November 1972	48-hour work stoppage	To abolish biannual claims negotiations, against repression, against subcontracting companies, to get rid of imperialism, in solidarity with miners, in solidarity with the martyrs of Cobriza, for job security, in support of metallurgical unions on strike
June 1973	24-hour work stoppage	Against government intervention of unions, in support of union of Sider-Perú and its fired workers, for withdrawal of police from Sider-Perú, for democratic elections in the fishermen's union of Chimbote, to repeal DL 19400 that created agrarian leagues, resolution of metallurgical strikes
August 1973	Metallurgical march	Repeal of DL 18471 of Labor Security Law, resolution of metallurgical industry conflicts, against government intervention in unions, freedom for detained union leaders, in solidarity with Vietnam
September 1973	Metallurgical march	In support of Chilean people, for political autonomy
December 1973	March	In support of unions in conflicts, for takeover without compensation of Cerro de Pasco mine

TABLE 2. *Continued*

Year	Event	Stated Objectives
March 1974	48-hour work stoppage	Against rising cost of living, for wage increases, against repression by employers and government, for rehiring of fired workers, against MLR, resolution of metallurgical industry conflict
August 1974	48-hour work stoppage	For rehiring of fired workers, for dismissing legal charges, against factory closures, against government intervention in unions, repudiation of MLR
September 1974	15-day strike staged by FETIMP	For rehiring of fired workers, for dismissing legal cases against leaders, against rising cost of living, for wage increases, against government intervention in unions, against plant closures and firings, against illegalization of strikes
April 1975	48-hour work stoppage	For rehiring of fired workers, for dismissing legal cases against leaders, for lifting of restrictions on civil liberties, against rising cost of living, against APRA and MLR
December 1975	Regional work stoppage staged by CGTP	Against massive firings in two companies: Plásticos El Pacífico and Record
February 1976	48-hour work stoppage	To abolish wage ceilings, to abolish limitations in negotiations
May 1976	FETIMP strike	For rehiring of fired workers, in support of Motor Perú union on strike, for job security, for wage negotiations without ceilings or limitations on bargaining
July 1977	General strike	Against repression and economic policies

The metallurgical unions engaged in radical collective action not only for the purpose of mutual aid but also to defend their common interests and protect the rights of all the unions. Unions acted together to defend endangered rights, which, in a direct and immediate way, concerned every union and every worker in the country. The defense of rights was a key issue in many of the cases that mobilized unions: the fight against the bi-annual negotiation of contracts in 1972; the struggle for the 1974 wage hike; the protest against the suspension of civil liberties in 1975; the resistance to wage ceilings in 1976; and the national strike of 1977.

The objectives that the metallurgical unions pursued through mobilizations and strikes made the state a focal point of the struggle. Unions forcefully demanded that the state respect their rights and pay attention to their claims. Placing the state at the center of a strategy of militant collective action is what gave the union movement in the metallurgical industry its clasista credentials.

In practice, a clasista union was, unequivocally, a combative union. As we have seen, however, it did not necessarily imply a clasista articulation of demands by the union. In reality, clasista meant that a union was prepared to enforce norms of reciprocity and cooperation that prevailed among unions in the struggle against the state. This action-oriented unionism developed during the military government of General Juan Velasco Alvarado. It was led by clasista union leaders and supported by leftist groups. Clasista leaders looked to leftist groups for guidance in the union struggles.

Union leaders acted as a "hinge" between the party and the workers. They guaranteed the influence of the party in the union. At the same time, they ensured the participation of workers in the struggles promoted and supported by the party. On its end, the party went to a lot of trouble to assure its ties to union leaders. Former leader Delmer Quiroz later observed that "the supposedly strong clasista movement inside the Federación de Trabajadores de la Industria Metalúrgica del Perú was not so. To a great extent, it was almost exclusively centered in its leadership's highest echelons."[2]

The relations between leftist parties and leaders were based on the support given by the party to the union and its leaders. In becoming party members, the workers also received ideological training. This made the link between the union and the party politically meaningful and reinforced the ties between the two.

Clasista leaders were exposed to the ideological influence of the party in political cell meetings. Those meetings, as Feliciano Pacheco related, "provided education to the worker so that he might realize to what social strata he belonged, if his situation was the result of bad luck or the product of the country's situation itself, if things were done by chance or were carefully prepared by the dominant groups." The ideological influence of the party extended well beyond the workers tied directly to the party. The core of party militants among union leaders in the factory had ties with a larger group of workers who were identified with the leaders and involved in the tasks of union organization. They made up what was recognized by the mass of workers as the clasista group within the factory. Union activity was directed and the rank-and-file worker was educated by this group. The vehicles for educating workers in the principles of clasismo were the union newspaper and speeches at union meetings.

The effects of this education showed up in the astonishing coherence in the views expressed by clasista workers. The former union leader Luis Helfers opined: "Many workers didn't realize that society as a whole, the system, everything basically revolved around the workers, the few of us who were conscious of this reality, knew that we were one of the main axes of society." Thus clasismo offered many workers a sense of playing a leading role in society, something that they lacked in everyday life.

The ideology of clasismo affirmed that political change was necessary to stop the exploitation of workers. Feliciano Pacheco, a former leader, said in this regard: "I think that a union isn't going to completely resolve the workers' key problems. Some of the benefits that came out of collective agreements, I think were short-term gains, but the increase in the country's economic crisis canceled out what was won and the workers went back to being exploited." Regarding the need for political transformation, clasismo identified the party as the vehicle that would lead the workers toward change. Affirming that workers were a social class was crucial to middle-class leftist groups because it validated the role of the party and its militants as leaders of a revolutionary class.

In the course of the ideological socialization that took place in the party, a hierarchical relationship between the politicized student and the activist worker was established. This reinforced the student's power and the worker's subordination. Life in the party cell was organized, to a certain extent, in the image of university life. Party members were expected to have a command of the language used in Marxist analysis. Young university students were experts in this, and that gave them a big advantage over workers in party matters. "It was necessary to have a grasp of the latest minutiae of a proposal in the party's program," the former leader Delmer Quiroz complained, "knowing almost by heart the classic texts of Marxism and handling a language which was, of course, far removed from that of the workers. Workers' circles were organized around the discussion of the latest party document and of certain classic texts, which were hardly read, but this allowed the leaders' groups to maintain hegemony."[3] In the leadership of the party, worker participation was always minimal.

The party membership of a worker allowed the party to control his behavior. From the sidelines, the party ensured that leaders stayed loyal to the union organization. As Baltazar Carpio, the leader of the Confederación General de Trabajadores del Perú, revealed, "If not for the party, workers cannot be disciplined." Through the party cell, the party controlled the conduct of the labor leader in coordinating activities with other unions. Interunion activity was of special interest because it was the arena in which parties of the Left competed for influence. In addition to the formal mechanisms, the personal relations among young activists and workers facilitated the exercise of control by the party. A former leftist activist related:

> One of the things I used to do as a militant was have long conversations with all the workers from the cell. If there hadn't been a friendly relationship, there wouldn't have been a political one. For example, somebody had to control a certain union leader who sometimes behaved in unpredictable ways. When he was elected as a delegate to a labor movement event, it meant a possibility for my party to have someone there to counteract the line of another political party at the event. I wouldn't have devoted so many hours to conversation with him if it weren't a political necessity. There was a closeness among us which made it possible to have a political relationship. On the basis of that relationship, he did everything I told him to do.

The subordination of the worker to the party allowed the party to realize its fundamental objective: preserving its influence over the union. It was essential that the governing board of the union be sympathetic to the political strategy of the party. For that purpose, it was important that the key posts be held by workers who were party members or by people whom the party trusted.

The link between the party and the union through a clasista leader made it possible for the union to make decisions on work actions or mobilizations to coincide with the party's strategy. Clasista leaders inside the factory indicated what work stoppages, strikes, and demonstrations workers were to undertake to support other unions or make alliances to defend common interests. What made workers respond to the calls of their leaders?

Calls that involved acts of solidarity with other metallurgical unions were almost unanimously accepted by the workers. Apparently, workers generally thought like the one who observed that "any Federación strike called in the name of solidarity was good." That was not the case, however, when it was a matter of support to unions outside of the metallurgical industry. In such cases, opinion would be divided. As former leader Feliciano Pacheco recalled, "Many compañeros didn't look favorably on this. They'd say, what do we have to do with workers from other sectors? We're metallurgical workers." At the same time, other workers did participate with a clasista conviction supporting such actions. The marches in support of the Chilean people were justified "because we all are brothers in the struggle of the people as proletarians," as Pedro Aguirre put it.

In addition to expressions of solidarity, unions called on workers to join in an "alliance for radical actions in defense of rights." Unions saw this as a strategy suited to the particular circumstances they faced—a situation in which a military government monopolized power and counted on the "passive support" of organized groups. Beginning in 1972, the government attempted to limit wage increases by introducing restrictions on union negotiations. In the previous four years, the union position had been strengthened as workers progressively won more rights. The repression of union activity gradually intensified, reflecting the extension of political repression across Peruvian society as a whole. Workers faced the challenge of organizing a united front to demand the lifting of restrictions on wage bargaining and to reject the limitations on union rights entailed in the government's suspension of civil liberties and outright intervention in some unions. But the participation of workers in antigovernment protests was not an automatic response by workers reacting to political repression. Union leaders explained that the way to defend benefits and rights was through collective action aimed at the government, not just at employers. They maintained that such collective displays of force by workers increased their ability to apply pressure in their respective factories. Workers who had the experience of acquiring rights through radical actions in the factory confirmed the efficacy of the strategy. The radicalism practiced collectively by unions in defense of principles and rights was understood by workers as an extension of the radicalism that was practiced at the factory level and part of the tradition of solidarity among unions. Thus there was a broad acceptance by workers of this radicalism, even among workers who were satisfied with specific government measures such as the job security legislation or who approved in general of the government. As one worker put it, it was government that "made the working-class brain wake up and begin to think about politics." "It was said that it was a dictatorship," Rolando Luzquiño said, "but that military government was okay; the measure to nationalize what the foreigners had was a step which satisfied us as Peruvians. I'd chat with my compañeros who said that the Agrarian Law was a good idea." That, however, did not keep Luzquiño from participating in antigovernment demonstrations because, as he himself recognized, "I saw that with the marches and the mobilization of all of us together that we'd achieve things."

For other workers, the specific ideological characteristics of the government were not of great interest. In fact, workers did not necessarily understand that the term "revisionist" shouted in slogans at different marches was a condemnation of the Communist Party's support of the military government. For many, the "revisionists" were simply the union rivals of their leaders, "the people who weren't in agreement with the policies of the union." Declining wages and the enactment of restrictions on collective bargaining eroded overall support for the military government. Political repression made it increasingly difficult for the union movement to pressure the government. Workers subsequently took the lead in the struggle against the military government that eventually ended in the transition to democracy in 1980.

The connections between leaders and workers in the individual unions in firms laid the foundation for workers' participation in class-based collective action. Union leaders dealt with workers who were mostly young and migrants. They benefited from the wage increases and protection that unions provided. The youth of the workers, along with the substantial wage increases won by the union, made these workers disposed to participate in acts of solidarity. They received no immediate rewards, but neither did their participation cost very much. Luzquiño recalled: "A forty-eight-hour work stoppage called by the Federación was a loss of pay for three shifts. You felt it if you lived off your wages, but for me it wasn't much of a sacrifice because I didn't have many responsibilities. Giving my support didn't cost me much because I was living with my parents and I had just recently gotten married two years before." On the other hand, supporting other unions or participating in marches and meetings with other workers was something requested by those same union leaders who successfully took charge of leading the battle to improve the workers' situation and protect them from abuses in the factory. The kindness and effectiveness of these union leaders evoked strong, permanent feelings of loyalty among workers. As one worker, Roberto Díaz, put it, "We didn't know what a political party was but we had good leadership. I became involved with the clasistas because of the good leadership." It is not surprising that workers repaid leaders for their loyalty to the union organization with a similar sense of loyalty. "The people," said Luzquiño, a worker who participated in the strikes and mobilizations and then stopped supporting the clasistas in the union, "had confidence in their leaders who would defend a worker even if he wasn't right. Then, when the union boss wanted to get out on strike, people supported it because they were good leaders and never let their guard down against the company." A leader would call the rank-and-file workers together and play on his influence over them, especially when he was asking them to participate in actions that could be more costly such as a prolonged strike. In these cases, it was not enough to have lower-ranking leaders or other clasista workers make the argument by appealing to the values and concepts of clasismo. It was necessary for the top-ranking union leader personally to get involved and display all his debating skills. Through such an exercise, the union leader reinforced the image of himself as the successful commander in the battles inside the factory. Some workers were swayed by a leader's call for participation because the leader implicitly appealed to their *trust* in him or because he inspired in them, to use the worker's word, sufficient *respect*.

Apart from loyalty or trust, the respect that workers felt for leaders also influenced their decisions to participate in the marches and meetings (like those for the celebration of May Day) to which they were called by the leaders. For the clasista leaders, the attendance of the workers at such events was especially important. Not only was it an expression of solidarity but the presence of workers in marches and their support for Federación-backed strikes served as visible evidence to leftist parties that leaders enjoyed the political backing of their workers. The leaders relied on this to enhance their status in the discussions and negotiations that went on among leftist groups inside the Federación. Such negotiations affected the partisan composition of the governing council of the Federación. "When there was a metallurgical march in order to protest the abuses of the employers," Braulio Vega, a former union leader, recalled, "we had to go out because over there in the Federación it also used to be a fight of political factions. Then you couldn't go alone without the rank and file, because then in whose name could you speak?" For workers, participation in these events was particularly stressful because it usually meant subjecting oneself to reprisals by the police. The probability of a violent response by police increased when university students participated in the marches and chanted antigovernment slogans. Some confessed that they discouraged students from coming to join in the marches, frightening them with warnings that the police had been instructed to attack them. That workers consented to participate in this high-risk activity was partially explained by a fear that was greater than their fear of police repression: the fear of what could happen to them if they did not participate. In other words, they feared losing the support of their union leader. Such support was crucial for protecting oneself in dealings with engineers and supervisors as well as for successfully applying for company benefits such as time off or loans. Nonparticipation put one's own union membership at risk. Anyone who did not go to a march or meeting had to excuse himself ahead of time. "Some compañeros who used to study at night," Feliciano Pacheco, a former secretary general of the union, related, "would show up and say, compañero, I'm studying and I can't attend, not because I don't want to but because I must be in class; in these cases there never was a problem." But in the cases when somebody stopped attending, Pacheco explained the consequences:

> Nonattendance was a reason for finger-pointing in the next assembly. You might be asked to say if you weren't in agreement [with the union] and if you said you weren't then you were told to resign from the union. Then the worker, looking for an excuse, would say, no, that my wife has been a little sick and I haven't been able to go. But for the next march that guy who had been pointed out had to show up and go. This was the kind of pressure that we'd put on people. Some would ask for expulsion, we'd say, compañeros, I think that this compañero here has the right to be given another chance. At that

time, to be expelled from the union was simply and plainly to be in the hands of the company and nobody wanted to be kicked out of the union, no one.

But aside from the loyalty or respect which the union leaders could inspire, union leaders used different coercive mechanisms to force the minority of workers that did not want to attend a march or meeting. Once the union decided to participate in an event, it was obligatory that all workers attend. The buses that transported workers in their daily commute would head to Plaza Dos de Mayo or another location. Once there, attendance would be taken and workers who skipped out were fined. "The leaders would give their speeches," a worker recalled, "and that's why you had to go. Now you wouldn't be going empty-handed, you had to go with your poster. You had to go. We'd arrive at the meeting point in the Plaza Unión, going from work, and the leaders would be there with the signs ready. Everybody would grab one. There would be people from APRA and they'd make you carry a placard and there were people who didn't like politics and they made them carry the signs anyway. This was the way to force us to get involved." Under these circumstances, workers found themselves demonstrating under the banners of partisan forces that they did not necessarily support. Máximo Chinga, a worker who supported the APRA party, was forced to show up as a demonstrator at the meeting of the leftist Unitario de Lucha carried out in Plaza San Martín in 1978. "That was a political meeting," Chinga complained, "and I argued that in that case, attendance shouldn't be required, but they didn't pay any attention to me. I was obliged to go because if you didn't go to a demonstration they'd fine you."

Whether out of respect, gratitude, or obligation, workers attended the marches and demonstrations largely on behalf of and for the union leader. No matter what their particular political convictions, workers sought to make good on their debts and obligations to leaders by their attendance at political events. So they would go, but after staying a short while, most would drop out and leave. Very few workers stayed for an entire event. Workers from the factory estimated that out of a total of 400 to 420 workers attending a demonstration, between 300 and 350 would leave before the event concluded. In the same way, workers went to marches trying to make sure that leaders knew they were there: "Many times I'd place myself at the head of the march," Jesús Zúñiga, a former union leader, remembered, "and our workers would always spread the word to let it be known that they were there."

Work stoppages, strikes, and demonstrations proved to be a weak basis for maintaining ongoing relationships among unions. As long as each union remained isolated and bargained individually with its respective employer, the success of the union movement depended on the ability of the union caudillos in the Federación to get individual unions to participate in collective action. When the union bosses left their posts, the clasista movement in the Federación Metalúrgica was weakened and unable to engage in militant collective action. Jaime Cáceres, the secretary general of the Federación Metalúrgica, reflected: "In reality, clasismo in the sector was quite dictatorial. The leading personalities of the workers' movement who were attached to the parties didn't represent an organized class consciousness. The top union bosses weren't an expression of that, but rather were leaders with personal ties to the masses, but once they were fired and removed from the leadership, the movement didn't last."[4]

The weakening of the movement was related to the departure of union caudillos, but the widespread firings in 1977 did not account for the leadership crisis. Rather, the logic of caudillismo in the labor movement unraveled as the bases of the relationship between union bosses and workers changed.

During the course of the 1970s, wages deteriorated and so did the relative cost of losing pay for each day on strike. Under these circumstances, workers' willingness to participate in strikes and work stoppages declined. Moreover, given the economic crisis, unions were not only unable to make gains but were losing ground in negotiations. As a result, workers no longer felt the need to repay leaders by mobilizing in response to their calls. Finally, the transition to democracy in 1980 made it unnecessary for unions to unite against the repressive and dictatorial measures taken to harm them.[5] These factors weighed heavily in the calculations of the workers from Metal Empresa who had found ways to get ahead other than relying on general wage increases. They realized that work stoppages in support of other unions were costly and that their own well-being was not greatly affected by acts of solidarity staged by other unions. With that realization, reciprocity between workers of Metal Empresa and other unions broke down. Other metallurgical unions followed suit. The Federación Metalúrgica's rapid ascent in the world of trade unionism was matched by its precipitous decline into oblivion.

This turn of events led some clasista leaders to critique the assumptions under which they had operated. They questioned the utility of having focused so much of their attention on union leaders so as to mobilize workers. They also questioned the emphasis on radicalism as an essential component of the clasista identity. Delmer Quiroz recognized that the weakening of clasismo did not begin with the firings of union leaders in 1977. According to him, a variety of problems became evident during the repressive phase of the military government—ranging from the lack of grassroots political work with the rank and file to the difficulties of rotating and recruiting leaders.[6] These weaknesses in clasismo had to do with how clasistas had conceived of the relationship between the party and workers. Quiroz observed that "political work focused too much on the leadership groups, on seeking political influence by winning posts such as that of secretary general, on just affiliating union leaders to the party."[7]

Some clasista leaders also questioned the emphasis on radical action as being synonymous with clasista political activity. Rather than equating politics with dramatic, radical action, these leaders saw politics as something that involved building consciousness and political capacity in the practices of everyday life. Divergent conceptions of politics divided some of the clasista union leaders from the party leaders who had a university background. Delmer Quiroz reflected on the different approaches to politics:

> Being clasista meant spreading the idea of all-out combativeness, but there was little generalized consciousness that the union organization is itself a valuable weapon, which you have to take care of, which you have to preserve, which you have to go on shoring up every day, that a union isn't only strong because it is able to call a strike today, that a union isn't only strong because it issues incendiary press releases, but a union is strong to the extent that all of its members share a basic consciousness: being fully conscious that it [unionism] is an earned right; that the strength of a union resides in the unity of its members, that there isn't any possibility of struggling for [individual] interest in an isolated manner; and once a step is taken you shouldn't go back, that it would be catastrophic to take one step back and therefore the steps should be careful, serious, taking care where you go backing down. That wasn't done. Clasista unions were trained to think that to be inside the prestigious circle of clasistas you had to sign all the com-

muniqués of the country. A union that did not appear in the famous declarations was a union of little prestige. To be strong, unions had to have brilliant leaders capable of engaging in polemics and seeming to be loud-mouthed. In order for the unions to be strong, they had to fall into line with every strike, and that was not even remotely true. It is more or less a question of understanding politics not as the will of four visionaries but as daily life, as the daily acts of people. That's politics![8]

The leaders also reviewed the relations they had maintained with the leftist parties and questioned the utility of involving workers in the "ideological fight between political parties," the "political cannibalism," and the "fight for control of the organizations." They complained about the lack of access to leaders, the vertical subordination of the union leaders to the party, and the way in which the party forced their removals on occasion.[9]

Many party members with a university background agreed with these criticisms. They too suffered from the continuing lack of internal democracy within parties and the divisive practices of their leaders. Like workers, party members simply deserted en masse from their political organizations, more often than not keeping their criticisms to themselves.

5
To Be a Worker Is Relative
Industry and the Limits
to (Re)Producing Workers

Amid favorable political conditions and growth in industrial production, the Metal Empresa union won concessions that increased the purchasing power of workers from 1970 to 1973. But workers' expectations were only partially satisfied. The wage scale in Metal Empresa — considered to be relatively high at the time — allowed each worker to cover the costs of daily expenses such as food, clothing, transportation, medicine, and school supplies. But it was insufficient for a family with many dependents. Neither did it permit a worker to realize one of his primary dreams: home ownership. Moreover, a portion of the regular expenses in the family budget could be covered only through additional pay for overtime work. As Jesús Zúñiga put it, overtime pay meant that you could "buy a shirt, a pair of pants, or send something to your family back in the countryside." Overtime pay was indispensable for covering part of the factory worker's normal expenses. While the wages at Metal Empresa might have appeared to be high in comparison with the pay at other companies, they were not high enough to cover the real costs of maintaining a household. Whenever union leaders sought to mobilize the workers against overtime by explaining to them in Marxist terms that it was really just another way to prolong the exploitation of the labor force and that workers had the right to rest and take care of their health, workers had a hard time understanding this theoretical jargon. The preaching against overtime failed.

Robinson Ledesma explained the problem of purchasing power in this way: "The wages didn't meet our needs. You couldn't own your own home, you had to go on paying rent. You couldn't have a set of household appliances either; neither a refrigerator nor a television set."

Moreover, workers were plagued by doubts about their long-term job security. Metal Empresa had been founded in the wake of the bankruptcy of the firm Promecán. That bankruptcy was a mystery to workers because they knew that the company had orders for products. The closing of Promecán left them skeptical about the notion of job security. "Before Metal Empresa"—Freddy Llamoca explained—"there was Promecán. Promecán closed just like that, while there was plenty of work, according to some co-workers who had been employed there. At the time, there were about fourteen ships being built but they closed anyway leaving the work unfinished." Metal Empresa itself never produced profits, thus creating nagging suspicions among workers. "Insecurity has been a continuing problem ever since the company was founded," Timoteo Calvo explained. "The company never had a year in which it declared a profit." The insecurity was fueled by the fact that no one knew for sure if new contracts would be forthcoming when the current production contracts ended. "It wasn't like the food industry," Robinson Ledesma said, "because everybody has to eat. Metals aren't the same, you can stop buying a metal frame window, but you can't stop eating. The company could decrease its production at any time. For example, when there was a contract with Mexico, that could last for a year and a half, but then there would be slack time afterward."

These circumstances forced workers to seek more income by going to great pains to take on any possible overtime shifts. And in some cases, workers planned and developed small-scale businesses in addition to their factory work. Some workers not only sought additional income through these independent ventures but saw them as a better alternative to factory work, or at least as a backup measure to protect themselves against unforeseen eventualities.

Workers like Justino Bautista, Jesús Zúñiga, and Celestino Peralta, who had large families to support, developed income-generating activities to augment their wages. Bautista had learned the tailor's trade and made shirts and pants at home. He explained, "I could never earn enough money." Because he was a union leader, Jesús Zúñiga often did not have the chance to earn overtime pay. To compensate, he would sell different items to his fellow plant workers such as combs, handkerchiefs, and ballpoint pens. In addition, in 1975, he opened a curbside stand in front of the factory where he sold breakfasts. He tried to open a beer store with Ramón Espinoza, another plant worker. Later on, he started a chicken ranch with Julio Salazar, a fellow factory worker. Zúñiga recalled:

Salazar had bought a plot of land. With seven thousand soles we bought all the stakes and mats and at night, after work at the factory, we made the chicken coops. Later, with our July bonus, we bought six thousand chickens, which arrived in little boxes, and we put a thousand chickens in each coop. While the chicks were still tiny, we got an offer to sell them and it was a good deal for us. But we began to think, If this is what they're offering us now, how much more might they offer us when the chicks are fully grown? So we didn't sell them, but it turns out that you have to give a lot of feed to chicks and we were running out of money. Then we began to borrow from everybody. We hit on everyone, even for the smallest sums, until we no longer had any place to go for a loan. A few days went by and the chicks didn't have any feed left when happily a few compañeros, who had gotten a loan from the company, gave us the money. With that we could finish fattening up the chicks. But as it turned out, when we tried to sell them, there wasn't anybody to buy them. Also as time went by, again, we didn't have any feed. Then we decided to go out and sell them ourselves. We put some chickens in a few sacks and went one Sunday to Acho to sell them. It was very sunny, we weren't selling many, and after a few hours the chickens started to smell bad. Somebody said to us, "Why don't you just give them away to the ladies from the neighborhood and get rid of them?" We went back to the farm and we didn't know what to do. Over the next few days, we went directly out to the Callao markets and they began to move until we sold all of them. When we finished, we had earned a profit. Then we paid all our debts and improved the chicken coops by putting in floors and lighting. With the experience we had, we thought this was going to turn out well. Chino [Salazar] said: "Look, if this turns out okay, to hell with the company, I'm quitting! Then you leave too and we'll make a fortune. We're killing ourselves for such assholes, why can't we just bust our butts for ourselves?" We bought six thousand more chickens and when we sold them, we made more money. Then Chino got a pickup truck for himself by making a down payment, for the purpose of delivering the chickens. But the third round turned out badly for us because the prices dropped and we lost money.

On another occasion, they let me in on forming a group with Valverde, Pacheco, Licona, and Peralta to set up a metallurgical workshop. We were all workers with on-the-job experience and the idea was to quit and use our severance pay to set up the business. But in the end, almost all chickened out and they didn't leave the factory. On another occasion, I bought two dollies for forty thousand soles and sold them for one hundred forty thousand. Then with Quiroz and Peralta, we bought a batch of stoves and we sold them. From there, I proposed buying a batch of scrap metal which Metal Empresa was selling. We submitted our letter with an offer of eighty cents per kilo but another person actually beat us out with a lower offer. Then Peralta said to me: "I can't go on here. I have six kids and we're never going to get ahead. Then, out of that, another idea for a workshop was born. The idea was to get out of the factory and with our severance pay, set up the shop. I said to him "Look, Flaco, since I'm a union leader, I can't quit. The one who has to quit is you." Then Flaco set out on his own. That was in 1976. Afterward, in 1977, I set up a restaurant in Rímac which my brother was managing, but it went broke. Also with Peralta, we bought a used truck from the shop, paying for it with a sixty thousand soles bank loan. I knew the engineer who was the owner of the shop, and he put a lot of trust in me. We used the truck for deliveries of iron and cement, and we contracted a driver who lived in Peralta's house and for his services he got free rent.

Other factory workers did not engage in activities of this sort, but they wanted to. "Since I had worked with my parents in the Callao marketplace until I was nineteen," Robinson Ledesma told me, "I saw that a grocery business was profitable and I wanted to start one but I didn't have enough capital. I had this desire to make more money. Besides, I always thought that the company wasn't very financially sound." One factor that revived plans for independent business activities among many factory workers was the extremely high incomes obtained in 1976. The economic windfall for workers was a product of the company's incentives policy that was applied to accelerate the completion of a shipbuilding contract for Mexico. Thanks to these incentives, workers earned incomes that were triple or quadruple their usual wages. This enabled many factory workers to realize their dream of building their own homes. In such matters, migrants distinguished themselves from Lima natives; some of the limeños preferred to use their extraordinarily high wages for other purchases, such as buying an automobile or vacationing.

From the standpoint of the workers' expectations and priorities, building a home was an extraordinarily important achievement. Esteban Vilcahuamán laid out his personal agenda: "In the first place, my goal was to build my own home, and in the second place, to buy the basic necessities for my home, and in the third place, to educate my children, so that in this way my children won't just go along like I had, right?" At the same time, having one's own home allowed one to plan a strategy for economic diversification. It provided an infrastructure that could be used to generate additional income by setting up some business at home or, in the last resort, using it for renting rooms. From another angle, having one's own home meant that extra income would not have to be spent on rent but could finance some other economic activity that eventually might let you leave the factory. "During that time," Esteban Vilcahuamán told me, "I put up my little house over there by Collique and I built my house and put a roof on it. I did it all with that [pay from that] work I had and then I practically didn't think about anything else except continuing to work in order to be able to get ahead and save some more money. I was thinking that after my house was finished, I would get enough money together to quit."

Justino Bautista considered the extraordinary income from the incentive plan to be temporary: "I thought that this was going to run out." He designed a complex strategy for economic diversification. He built a two-story house on Rímac Beach. The first floor was divided into two units: one for a grocery store run by his wife and the other for a restaurant. In addition, he acquired a stand in the market and planned to set up a workshop once the incentives policies gave him enough to purchase tools. The incentives did not continue long enough to fund his tool purchase. Bautista offered to quit the company but asked for a sum in severance pay that would have been enough to start the shop. The company refused his proposal. In addition, he had to shut down the store after a time because of excessive competition in the neighborhood. The restaurant never worked out. A few years later, with his situation deteriorating, Bautista set the second floor of his house aside for renting rooms. He planned to reopen the market stand, which had remained closed. He reconfigured the space originally intended for the restaurant as a car wash. His oldest son, who was an unemployed worker, was put in charge. In addition, he raised two rams outdoors behind his house.

By itself, a factory wage was not sufficient to cover the costs of maintaining a worker and his family. Migrant serranos diversified by seeking out different sources of income. To a certain extent, the activities were an urban imitation of the Andean economy. Using his wages, Bautista put up a dwelling with a space for small business and set up a market stand. These activities were supposed to generate enough capital to finance a second stage: namely, a workshop. Clearly, he was engaged in an economic strategy in which resources were not concentrated in any single activity. To minimize risk, they were spread across different venues (a factory, store, restaurant, and market, almost mimicking the multileveled terrace cultivation of land on an Andean mountainside): if the income in one place went down, it would be compensated by income from somewhere else. In Bautista's project, the store and workshop went hand in hand, and the rental income compensated for wage reductions. At one point, the diversification of resources could have made possible a growth and capitalization strategy revolving around the small workshop. Later, the diversification of resources took on a defensive function, allowing Bautista to devise a more complex survival strategy.

Given the inadequate wages and insecurities associated with factory employment, it was not surprising that workers did not resist or oppose the downsizing proposed by the company in 1977. Rather, they were inclined to take advantage of the bonus offered by the company in order to quit. They did so with the idea of setting up their own businesses. One official informed the company's board of directors that "the restructuring of the tenured plant personnel [was done] within an atmosphere of complete harmony." "The desire to leave," Timoteo Calvo, a former leader, explained, "was apparent during the downsizing. We'd try to stop people from leaving and many told us that they would prefer to leave the factory because they had planned to set up a business or a little store; others wanted to go to Venezuela; and others were demoralized because there was a period of about a year and a half in which they had very little to do on the job."

Most of the workers who quit the company are now engaged in independent ventures. Out of the sixty workers who left Metal Empresa, the largest group consisted of those who had taken advantage of the skill they had learned and then had set up workshops or contracted out their services in the metallurgical field. The rest were in other businesses and different

TABLE 3. *Economic Activities Undertaken by Sixty Retired Metal Empresa Workers*

INDEPENDENT ACTIVITIES

Workshops and Services in the Metallurgical Industry (total number of workers = 12)

 Door and window workshop in Carmen de la Legua

 Garage in Callao

 Lathe shop in Comas

 Contractor in metal assembly and shop in Caja de Agua

 Lathe shop and locksmith's shop in Comas

 Independent boiler repair

 Metal products workshop in Callao

 Metal products workshop in Callao

 Soldering workshop in Comas

 Lathe shop in Surquillo

 Metallurgical workshop

 Locksmith's shop

Business and Various Services (total number of workers = 24)

 Thread and button wholesaler

 Food wholesaler warehouse in Surquillo

 Two bars (in Chacra Colorada and Chimbote) and contractor for naval repairs
  in Chimbote

 Market shoe stall in Tumbes

 Radio engineering workshop in Huancané

 Shoe repair shop

 Bookstore in Zárate

 Street fruit vendor in Callao (with four pushcarts)

 Owner of two bakeries

 Beer distribution (with own truck)

 Two buses on the Lima-Callao route

 A bus

 Two buses on the Comas–Año Nuevo route

 Music group in Ventanilla

 Music group

 Taxi drivers (8)

METALLURGICAL WORKERS (total number of workers = 19)

 Contract work in Venezuela (5)

 SIMA workers (4); one after the failure of his furniture business

 INSA workers (3)

 TRADECO worker (1)

 Temporary workers (4); one after the failure of his shop

 Workshop workers (2); one after selling clothing

TABLE 3. *Continued*

VARIOUS (total number of workers = 5)
Consultant on union activities
Highway toll collector
Door-to-door plumber
Failed chicken farm, moved to Chimbote
Unemployed

---

independent services. Others had gone back to being industrial workers and, in some cases, then attempted to start up independent businesses (see Table 3).

As their purchasing power deteriorated, other workers also made plans to quit, but many were not able to carry them out. As Braulio Vega told it, "When things began to get worse under the Morales Bermúdez government, I began to think about quitting. I had the idea of getting out with my brother-in-law and buying a minibus. But I didn't have enough with what we were making and I had doubts and so we didn't leave. If I had decided to do so at that time, I don't know how I'd be doing now."

Notably, the workers who tended to develop activities that they combined with factory wage earning were the serranos. Given the limits on wage earning, these workers sought supplemental income and even full-time alternatives to factory work. The cases already discussed—Pacheco, Zúñiga, Salazar, Peralta, Bautista—are all those of serranos. On the other hand, out of a group of twenty-eight workers who currently work at the plant and receive regular incomes from sources outside of the factory, twenty-three are serranos and five are from the coast.[1]

The migrant serranos had developed a sense of how to overcome the limitations posed by the environment. When a migrant moved to Lima, he was separated from his hometown by more than physical distance. The move was also a rejection of the stagnation of provincial life and a search to break away from it and to progress in life. Progress meant change and constantly bettering oneself. In the words of Esteban Vilcahuamán, to make progress is—like migrating—"to walk a little farther and not stay in the same place." Migration itself became a model of successive changes made in the service of this personal vision of getting ahead. In the process, the migrant ceased to identify himself with his original community. In the long or short run, the migrants came to think of the people from their hometowns as "the others" or "them." After a few years in the city, Esteban Vilcahuamán returned to Chilca in Huancayo province, feeling different: "I was stuck my whole life on a small farm and that was it. They weren't interested in anything else but keeping up the farm day to day and having enough to eat and nothing more." In the eyes of a limeño, a migrant from the provinces is just a "serrano." But in reality, he is not just that; he is no longer just your average country bumpkin, just as he is not a limeño either; he is different, he is a "migrant."

The serrano's quest for progress is the pursuit of an ideal. That ideal stands in contrast to everything that is missing in his life. The ideal is to achieve economic security and independence in one's own business. The ideal may not be explicit when a migrant first moves, but it unfolds as he becomes incorporated into urban life. The intense attachment to this ideal allowed migrants to view industrial work as a way station on the journey to get ahead. Esteban Vilcahuamán observed:

> If we leave our hometowns to get ahead, we're like the Chinese. If the Chinese come to the capital or any other place, surely they're going to start an industry or a business. They're thinking about setting up a sound and profitable one and when they already have something, something good, they go back to their place of origin and enjoy their money the best way they can. That's the way we are, too. We crap in our pants working, but we do it and we have something, indeed that's the way it is. A serrano does not show up just to work but he comes with an eye to getting ahead. That's exactly why some get factory jobs, with this view because most are thinking about working first to get capital and then to become independent by themselves.

This opinion was shared by workers from Lima. Luis Helfers concurred:

> The country folk, from the moment they come to work, the serranos cultivate the idea of working independently, of having their own little shop, their own pushcart, their own business. So each time a serrano shows up here, from the start, he gets in wherever he may, as a helper, a waiter, whatever. He soaks up all he can wherever he gets in to learn anything stupid to compete with the other asshole. The one who starts as a waiter is already thinking about how to set up an inn, a restaurant, or a pushcart. He puts up a Chinese take-out joint in

Plaza Unión, a few noodles, what the hell, he puts it all together like the best Chinese restaurants. He has a few big pans and he tosses [the noodles] up to the roof and he doesn't even drop a noodle.

Serranos distinguished themselves from the criollos in their attitudes toward work. The criollo workers, like Carlos Hidalgo, recognized that "the goal of having a little store or small business mostly comes from the serrano workers. Me, for example, what I aspire to, is having my own home and comforts: my furniture, a refrigerator, my television set, and that's it." Esteban Vilcahuamán observed: "In the criollo's case, I have never seen an eye toward wanting to get ahead. I've never seen it. It's only a matter of wanting to live better or wanting to be better off. That's what I've always seen. But wanting to put together your own capital and your own organization to better your lot in life, I've never seen that strictly speaking. You can say it's so because they [criollos] only want to enjoy life and that's it. They're never worried about their advancement but on the other hand, for the serranos, yes, it's very different."

From the very beginning, some migrant serranos who started in Metal Empresa had a long-term goal of owning a business. Even before working at Metal Empresa, Esteban Vilcahuamán harbored the idea of starting a business. Throughout the course of holding many different jobs, he came to the conclusion that "upon seeing companies doing so well, I thought about getting together a little capital and starting my own company by myself." When he left Promecán in 1968, he started a small business selling meat with his wife. He explained: "I really tried to improvise in the business and in other things, right? To get ahead is something I've always liked and that is precisely why I went into that meat business." He had to get out of the meat business because of problems with the license and he took a job at Metal Empresa, but not with the idea of staying for long. "My intention was to learn to work with metal because, I was thinking, right? From the time I began to work in construction, I was thinking about starting some small companies in order to be able to support myself and overcome things." Jesús Zúñiga had the same goal when he started at Metal Empresa: "My ambition was to be a great businessman. From the time I was very small I had worked in a restaurant business in San Juan de Lucanas. When I arrived in Lima, the old man at the food stand where I was working was a very hard worker. He would get up at 4:00 in the morning to prepare his roast and he would go to bed at 11:00 at night. He ended up with three houses and at each one he would raise chickens and pigs. I suppose that all of that has influenced me to want to be a businessman."

The migrant threw himself into a situation of uncertainty when he moved to Lima, where getting ahead depended on oneself. In contrast, limeños could use their clientelistic ties to local notables in Lima. The migrant could rely only on his own drive to work. It was a drive acquired early in life and it was indispensable for making one's way in an environment where the migrant could feel as foreign as an immigrant from China. The clarity of the serrano commitment to work was identified as a distinctive virtue. "The serrano never drags his feet," Esteban Vilcahuamán said, "but he lifts himself up by his own bootstraps." Not everyone was equally successful in this dramatic effort; some failed in making the adjustment altogether. Overwhelmed by stress, some migrants made use of the psychiatric services at the Hospital Obrero (Workers' Hospital). They were issued medical certificates recommending that they leave the city for health reasons. This relieved migrants of some of the guilt they felt in failing at city life and made it easier to return to their communities.[2]

To get ahead, the migrant organized his daily schedule in the city in a manner reminiscent of peasant life. Every day was completely devoted to work in a variety of diverse settings. His life did not follow a normal sequence of studying and then working, but rather the migrant worked and studied at the same time. His day was devoted to varied pursuits: working, studying, dedicating himself to some casual job or business, building a house, or doing domestic chores. At one stage, Jesús Zúñiga was working in a factory while at the same time leading the union, supervising his food stand business in front of the factory, attending party meetings at night, and building coops for a chicken farm which he had set up with another worker. In the view of Feliciano Pacheco, the limeños were lazy because they did not work on Sundays or holidays. "The provincial compañero is told that he has to work on a Sunday for the whole day or on a holiday and he just does it without qualms. On the other hand, I've seen compañeros from Lima who wouldn't sacrifice their Sunday. They'd prefer to rest or they already had plans made."

Migrants had another useful trait that was rooted in the peasant experience: the capacity to delay gratification. That tradition of delayed gratification endowed the migrant with a quality that was crucial for personal advancement: the ability to wait. Even in the toughest times, a migrant was capable of saving by engaging in economic activities in the home or elsewhere. He also demonstrated unusual foresight. Freddy Llamoca saved part of his wages from 1977 and onward—even though the purchasing power of his wages was declining—in order to acquire a stall in the marketplace. He did this in anticipation of any eventual closing of the company. Another exceptional case was that of Hercilio Carhuancho. For years, he devoted himself to buying up the largest possible quantity of school notebooks that the company sold at cost to workers. When he left, he had accumulated such a large quantity of notebooks that he set up a stationery store.

"The person from the country is a saver. He looks forward to saving in order to buy things for himself," Feliciano Pacheco pointed out. In this sense, the serrano also feels different from the criollo, who "looks for ways to amuse himself, have a good time, and ends his week between Saturday and Sunday and by Monday has only enough money left for bus fare." One of the priorities for saving extra income is for a home. Esteban Vilcahuamán related his views on the problems of criollos:

> Conversing with a criollo, I'd say to him, look, see, you say that you don't have enough money but the fact is that you go to the bars, you start drinking, you go out to have a good life, and of course you don't have enough. Then I ask you, look, see, you're very smart, very learned, intelligent but even though you're intelligent because you know a lot, you're an asshole, I tell him. But why? he asks me. Look brother, I'm telling you, a serrano who comes here to the capital, you won't ever see him just sitting in his house, he may be sitting on a brick or a wooden chair if possible, but he has something to sit on. But you see a criollo who thinks he knows a lot but, sometimes, unfortunately, he doesn't even have a place in which to sit down? You [guys] only look for a way to dress up nice and the women look to wear make-up and all of that and you think that with this you're doing something good. But in my opinion, I don't think so. Can you trade artificial beauty for the real thing? You can't, and one other thing then. Look, you dress well and wear good shoes. You live well. You have a television set but your life isn't all right. The serrano who knows how to think, yes, he does have a good life even though it might be on a little scrap of land, but he has one. But on the other hand, a criollo can be living for years in the same rented house with

his mother, his father, his grandfather, and his great-grandfather. But still, they're criollos. Unfortunately, what I see are not criollos but fools.

Luis Helfers, a criollo, put it this way:

For the criollo, money is for spending. The serrano counts each coin in his change. He's capable of missing his own bus stop just to make sure that he gets his change back. The criollo won't do that. He makes a feint at the driver and says to him: "I know you man, I've got your number. The next time I'll take your head off," but he doesn't miss the stop to get his change back. He doesn't do so because he doesn't want to walk any farther. The serrano doesn't have anywhere to sit down, he doesn't have any chairs, he has a piss-poor kitchen, his clothes are ragged, he wears used or donated clothes, but he has all his money. The criollo looks forward to having his own car and putting on nice clothes, stylish duds, good clothing, and sometimes I myself have ordered custom-made calf leather shoes. You had to look good to get a good job. You know that they say that appearance is everything.

Consumption versus savings, short term versus long term, immediate satisfaction versus delayed gratification—these were the opposing poles on a cultural spectrum that distinguished the fading criollo caste from the serrano migrants who, it seemed, made their way in life by constant effort.

The drive for self-improvement ultimately was fruitful for serranos like Jesús Zúñiga. Like others, he left the factory to devote himself to a business. Like his counterparts, he looked at the future from a new vantage point:

I think the country is entering a new phase in which serranos and provincial people have begun to take the first steps toward not only leading a union but also of being able to run a shop or a company. Right now, most of us are crawling. But those who will come after us will come with a different outlook and, in that sense, with new hope for the future in Peru. All these people, in new places, and by the hundreds, are working on their own. A time is going to come, and I hope it is soon, when there are new prospects for national industry and for decentralized development.

6

Amid Frustration, Indignation, and Fear

The workers who chose to remain at Metal Empresa pinned their hopes on the job security associated with industrial work. Nonetheless, in the years that followed, workers found themselves confronting a drastic, inflation-induced reduction in real wages and wage increases negotiated in collective bargaining that did not make up for their losses. At the same time, employers breached collective contracts in ways that further reduced workers' benefits. Pondering the situation, Walter Huatuco reflected: "What being a worker means is that there's impoverishment. The trick lay in attempting to survive in the crisis. Now, it's no longer a good deal to be a worker."

According to workers, their 1984 weekly income from wages of seventy thousand soles allowed them to cover their grocery bills for only three or four days. Consequently, they had to use their wits to survive. They sought out supplementary income through one or more of the following strategies:

1. Extending the workday in activities outside of the factory
On the basis of information provided by some of my factory informants, I identified a group of twenty-eight workers (by no means a majority) who had regular income apart from their wages. These were workers who generated additional income through extra work. For example, four workers took up taxi driving. One worker did radio-electronic repairs while another did auto body painting. Workers in this group were also found doing odd jobs in welding, locksmith work, and boiler repair. They found these jobs in workshops, the neighborhood, or in small subcontracting companies.

2. Generating income through activities, financed by factory wages, under the direction of another person
In this group, there were nine workers with grocery stores, three workers with minibuses, two workers with beer stores, two workers with metallur-

gical shops, one worker with a clothing shop, one worker with a market stall, and one worker who rented his car as a taxi. A typical example of a worker using this strategy was Gerard Aerate. He owned a motor repair shop a block away from the factory that was run by his son.

3. Using domestic infrastructure for generating income

The clearest case of the application of this approach is that of two workers from the group of twenty-eight who rented rooms in their houses. But this strategy usually accompanied the preceding strategy as in the case of grocery store operators who used part of their living quarters for the business.

4. Supplementing income through the activities of other family members, usually wives and children

Undertaking any of the above strategies was based on having achieved access to certain resources in the urban economy. A skilled worker had the know-how to be an independent tradesman. Acquiring a plot of land through a squatters' invasion, building a home, or landing a stall in the marketplace endowed a family with a potential source of additional income. Some individual strategies were relatively simple. This was the case of the workers who used their skills in part-time jobs such as making iron doors and windows for their neighbors. Another example was that of a worker from Lima who earned forty thousand additional soles per week in 1984 by turning his automobile into a taxi. But he did so only occasionally. He explained: "I don't always go out, except when I'm desperate for money, otherwise I go to play football or to rest." Such logic would have seemed strange to a serrano.

Others devised individual approaches that were a little more complex, combining wages with more than one basic survival strategy. For example, one worker extended his workday and rented a room in his house. Along with his 1984 weekly income of seventy thousand soles, he received fifty thousand soles from a tenant who rented a room in his house. Nine times that year, he took part-time jobs in welding, earning around sixty thousand soles for each job.

The most complicated individual approaches or those with most diverse sources of income were based on a broad integration of family members. Such a strategy might involve aggregating supplementary incomes or a more complex variant of mounting economic activities based on common family resources. The family of Pedro Aguilar provides an example of income integration based on diverse sources. In 1984, the

Aguilar family supported itself on four incomes: that of the wife (a seam-stress), the twenty-four-year-old son (a security guard), and the twenty-three-year-old daughter (an executive secretary). In the case of Feliciano Choque's family, income in addition to wages came from other family members who supported themselves on family resources. Feliciano's wife ran a stand in the market acquired with money from company bonuses. His son's dry cleaning shop was set up in a part of the house. Income was also derived from renting rooms on the second floor. Another possible way of diversifying the sources of a family income was by forming rela-tionships in the neighborhood community. This was the case of a worker named Percy Hinojosa, who organized a cooperative with his neighbors. Together they acquired a plot of land which they set up as a market where each one of the partners had a stand. In times of great need, the extended families of brothers and sisters also got involved to support fellow family members.

Workers were forced to spend most of their money on food. This prac-tically eliminated any budget for clothing and entertainment and limited the amount of spending on transportation. At the same time, working-class families cut back on the quality and quantity of foods consumed. Workers who could not rely on family support suffered to an even greater degree.

The changing quality of working-class life in the 1980s was described poignantly by Eugenio Vilcapoma. Eugenio had two children. He was able to cover his family's expenses with income from a meat vending stand which his wife managed. But he separated from his wife and was left with only his wages to support himself and his children. Then, as he recalled, "from the moment I've been here on my own, well, I've been really having a horrible life." Between 1980 and 1984, he stopped buying clothes. Apart from indispensable expenses like water and electricity, he bought only food. As he put it, "I supported only my stomach and nothing else, just imagine." He also cut back on meals and significantly modified his diet. He would buy less meat, potatoes, green vegetables, milk, and fish. The family even changed their favorite dishes and customs at social celebra-tions. He described the deterioration in household consumption:

> We have changed our cooking because before we'd make soup, a main course, and something for dessert, right? And so on, but now no. In contrast, now it's very different. In order to cope with our situation,

we make one thing. We make soup for one whole day. The next day it's a main course, dessert only once in a while. If there's enough money, there's a snack but if there isn't, none. In this situation, you have to count your money in order to be able to survive. For example, meat. We have meat only twice a week, once, or three times, and that's just one example. Let's take another: potatoes for example, which I like so much. Before we used to buy five, six, seven, up to ten kilos for the week, but now we buy three or four kilos per week. What do we do now? Then, in order to fill your belly, as they say, you buy something else. You buy something like wheat bran with a little bit more rice.

Before we used to buy quantities of green vegetables, for example, such as peas, corn, lima beans, and so on, right? So as to be able to eat them in a stew, really a soup with a lot of things thrown in. Or if not that, your spicy beans with meat, everything, right? But not any more, it's very different, meat is like a seasoning for food and nothing else. I don't buy any milk because I don't know what kind of milk it is; bitter, or rich, or sweet, I don't know. I don't know what milk is like. The only thing I do is I sometimes go to the store and buy powdered milk and that's so that I can imagine I'm drinking milk and that's it, but really I don't drink milk. That's the truth, huh? It's true.

Bonito [a saltwater fish similar to tuna], in 1964–65, it was a fabulous year, right? Bonito used to be the food of the poor, indeed it used to be their food or it might be eaten by the serranos who would come down from the hills. Everybody would throw in a little bonito in their meal, huh? In their soup, in their sweet potatoes, a little bit of it with some other fish and that's it. Well, it used to be the food of the poor. But nowadays you don't ever see bonito and if you do see it in the plaza they're now selling it by kilos, 2,800 soles for a kilo of bonito. Just think. Apart from all that, they weigh bonito with everything, with guts and all, no? With all the filth that it has. They don't even take it out or clean it at all. What are they doing? You can't really eat it anymore. A bonito weighs at least, okay, some weigh three kilos, four kilos, right? And how much is it going to cost you? Twelve thousand, thirteen, eight, nine thousand. A person who earns less and less can no longer get that seafood. Usually they look at it and that's it. They can only sigh, or let tears fall down their faces.

Imagine! Beans, the canary beans that the criollos never wanted to eat. That's what serranos eat and nobody else, they used to say. But now I've seen things on several occasions from the standpoint of a poor person, the way I'm now, right? I've gone to several gatherings at friends' houses or through friends of friends who would invite me and when I've gone they now serve everyday dishes like they are even a delicacy. For example, once a friend was going to give a dinner for a compañero, okay, and I went, right? We went and honestly they served us a big plate of beans with goat's meat that they called goat's stew. Just imagine, before it didn't use to be this way but rather it would be with turkey, chicken, or mutton. At least you'd have dry potatoes or a dish of spiced meat, something you didn't have every day. But now, no. It's only everyday food for festivals or birthdays maybe, the spicy goat meat, or maybe chicken or pork.

It's even the same when you go to a birthday party. One time I went to one around Santa Anita because it was also a get-together. The guy was from Chiclacayo. So I went there and they gave me, what do you call it? *Olluquito con charqui* [a traditional dish of tubers with dried meat] at a birthday party. They gave me beef strips, but of course there was more olluquito than beef, right? as if it were more meat that way. It was pretty much everyday food. That has really become the favorite meal for gatherings. So I see what it's like now, right? Now in comparison with before it is very different. A lot has changed. Before, what did we used to drink? The people usually drank beer. Whoever came to visit brought a case or two cases of beer. But today, you only say, "Congratulations on your birthday and another year of life, brother." There's a hug and nothing else and the person who comes doesn't bring a gift either, huh? And before, that didn't happen. Whoever came, would come with a gift. He'd come sometimes bringing a suit, or at times a cut of cloth or material or maybe bring underwear, a jacket, or a sweater, or some shoes, right? And it was like that, compañero, it used to be nice to celebrate a birthday, but not any more. That's all over now. Only people who have money can celebrate their birthdays and those who don't have any, don't. We stopped buying many things. So now, it's being able to survive, as far as I can tell. Since I see my compañeros who also are living in the same situation, and I ask one or another, they're also living about the same and they're doing just about the same thing to get by. What do they do? They turn to other things and they can't come up with enough food either and then their children are also really beginning to become malnourished, I see it myself. What can I do?

Other workers also described changes in their eating habits. Pérez related, "Before, my children used to eat eggs, but now you have to throw together a soup from bones." Percy Hinojosa also had to cut down on family visits. He explained: "Many times you have to deprive yourself of the habits which you had before, right? Like going out to visit the family in order not to spend now on bus fares and also when you do visit a relative, you can't go empty-handed because you're always supposed to take them something. So sometimes you have to avoid this, clearly forbidding family visits even to your brother's house."

In 1983, the business situation of Metal Empresa plunged workers into a permanent state of uncertainty; they contemplated the prospect of a possible plant closure. They feared losing their jobs and their benefits. The situation in Metal Empresa and other metallurgical plants was such that, according to Walter Huatuco, "it's frustrating being a worker because you think: this job isn't going to last for me." The worker lost confidence that his situation as a worker could at least assure him of a future with job security. "Before," Timoteo Calvo said, "getting a job in the factory used to be the best thing you could have and you'd be happy. You used to think that your future was assured for you and your family. Now, skepticism has grown. That worker who used to think about having a secure future and lending a hand to his family, that worker knows today that he's destroyed, demoralized. He no longer feels secure enough to confront problems. His impotency is now a psychological phenomenon that makes him ill. He belongs to a trapped, frightened social class. The principal preoccupation of people is whether they're going to be paid next week or not, if the company is even going to exist next month or not."

Going to work at the factory became a boring, frustrating routine, unbearable for workers. "When there used to be plenty of work," Vilcapoma recalled, "it was very nice and calm, you'd forget everything, you'd only concentrate on your job and just on getting your piece done, a perfect piece of equipment, a fine piece of work, and that was enough to calm you down. But when there isn't any work, when they take our work away and they don't pay us our benefits, you start thinking, everything worries you; then the situation is no longer normal; then you feel as if you're sick, mentally ill."

That fear of losing the job dampened the enthusiasm for making demands on the company. "There are workers who say that it's not necessary to ask for much of a raise," Bartolomé Valverde, a union leader, observed, "because the company is going broke and we'll end up on the street." To keep their jobs, workers did tasks that were not part of their normal duties. "Sometimes it happens," Timoteo Calvo explained, "that a boilermaker is sent to clean rest rooms and does so without protesting." At the same time, going to a lot of trouble to get a promotion made no sense because, given the low level of wages, promotions became meaningless. When mistreatment by bosses did occur, workers felt defenseless.

One of the workers' greatest fears was that the company's deteriorating financial situation would compromise the payment of fringe benefits. Indeed, some workers who wanted to quit as soon as possible could not do so because the company would withhold their benefits. Eugenio Vilcapoma complained about this. To prevent his children from becoming malnourished, he tried to quit to set up a produce store so that his children could at least eat the unsold vegetables. He was unable to do so. "Since I don't have any capital," he explained, "what can I do? A guy without money isn't worth anything."

Workers were nostalgic about their lost security and status. They realized that more and more self-employed workers—even those hawking skin creams on the street—had better incomes than they did. Percy Lescano reflected: "Today, it's different; the thing is to go out to seek your fortune wherever it might be. Today there is no longer a place for shame. Now, what a person looks for is to survive, working in whatever it might be. Today there are no longer barriers to that. I asked a skin cream vendor and then a snow cone vendor how much they earn. They take home about twenty thousand soles per day. They earn more than I do! I think the worker has chosen to be a street vendor because, although it's insecure, it leaves you with something to live on."

But workers also recognized that the conditions outside the factory were more difficult than a few years earlier when other workers from the company quit to venture forth in independent businesses. Their evaluations drew on their knowledge of the experiences of workers who had failed in their attempt to set up businesses. In the face of a prospective plant closure, however, a worker had no choice but to think about undertaking some independent activity. A metal repair shop, a painting shop, a carpentry shop, a market stand, a produce store—these were some of the possibilities they entertained in their daily conversations. Continuing in industry was no longer possible because of the low wages and growing unemployment. They did not want to find themselves, as Vilcapoma put it, "running up against the same situation" in the future.

More than ever, they did not want their children to be workers. Walter Huatuco explained the reasoning: "Because they're going to suffer like us, they're not going to pay them their hours; they're going to close the factory on them; they're not going to find another job." They wanted their children to study and overcome the conditions in which they had had to live. Workers who had adolescent children began to think more about the future of their children than about their own. They looked on their own efforts with the same sensibility that was expressed by Conrado Reyes: "My relief is [in knowing] that I'm trying to help my children get ahead because the only legacy which I can leave them is an education, right? or maybe a profession or something."

Union activity in the 1980s focused on reacting to the company's maneuvers with radical rhetoric and action. The company's chronic noncompliance with labor agreements added to the problems associated with low wages and the uncertainty about future job security. In the early 1980s, the company was no longer living up to the provisions laid out in the collective contract that had been negotiated with the union. The company failed to provide work clothes (overalls and shoes), personal care supplies (detergent, toilet paper, soap), travel allowances, loans, and indemnification advances. Moreover, the company stopped making social security contributions, which prevented the workers from using the medical services provided by the social security agency.

The cuts in workers' benefits took place in the climate of distrust that had shaped the relations between the union and the company. For the union, the company's noncompliance with agreements was simply an "employer's provocation." "They don't keep their collective bargaining agreements," declared the union newspaper *Labor Clasista* in February 1981, "claiming that the company is suffering its worst economic crisis in history without recalling that this has always been the same old story." In 1984 a union leader observed, "We can't believe that a multinational corporation like Metal Empresa is in this situation; perhaps a smaller company, but not Metal Empresa." This conclusion was shared by rank-and-file workers like Modesto Campos, who speculated, "Any job we do is for millions [of soles], but that money, where is it?" On the other hand,

some other workers thought that the situation went beyond the company's exclusive responsibility. This was the case of Pedro López: "In my
view, there's no alternative for curing this ill. What is required is an emergency plan for industrial reactivation. We don't think so much that the current situation may be a company maneuver, but rather that it's economic
policy." Certainly for the company officials, noncompliance with agreements was the direct result of the industry's situation during the second
Belaúnde administration. As one company official observed:

> The military leaders made many mistakes, but all of them together
> had coherence. The current [functionaries] are very intelligent, edu-
> cated in Chicago or in Boston, and each one of their measures in
> isolation is very smart, but all of them together are incoherent. In
> the previous economic model neither labor stability nor the bene-
> fits agreed upon with the workers got in the way. There were tax
> incentives, incentives for exports, and low taxes for the purchase
> of supplies. Recently, trade was liberalized but at the same time
> labor stability was maintained. Now some one hundred million soles
> to comply with the benefits provisions for two hundred thousand
> workers is a lot of money. The situation only provides leeway for the
> company to keep its doors open and meet the payroll. We explained
> this to the union but the union said "false"; if we put out the figures
> they say that the company must have its real bookkeeping under the
> table.

The company itself, however, fueled this distrust. In February 1982, the
union requested a review of the company's contracts, seeking information
regarding the firm's real financial situation. The company refused to share
the information with the union.

Reasons to distrust the company increased as job security itself came
into question. In 1984, the union concluded that the company's plan to sell
a twenty-thousand-meter lot was possibly a new "employer's maneuver."
In the view of union leaders, the purpose of the land sale was to create
another enterprise adjacent to the factory that would employ nonunionized labor. "The company wants to destroy the rights won and start again
on new ground," the leaders told me. This opinion was shared by workers
like Eugenio Vilcapoma, for whom "the same companies seek to destroy
the union, because there is work. The company is trying to destroy the
union in order to be able to exploit people again in order not to pay so

many benefits which we had gotten from them. I think they want to go back to another time. Then all the companies make it appear as if they don't have work."

Frustrated by the severe erosion of workers' rights and distrustful of the company's explanations, the union held the company fully accountable for the situation. As evidenced in the social and political violence in Peru in the 1980s, force was frequently used to settle conflicts. This violent reactive behavior was not invented by workers; it was a lesson they learned from the state, starting with the government of General Morales Bermúdez, who had union leaders fired in retaliation for the July 1977 national strike.

On the union side, threatening language was used to suggest that violence might be employed in resolving conflicts. During collective bargaining negotiations in 1980, the union pointed out in its newspaper that workers would defend their rights "with their lives." In the same vein, when faced with the company's attempt only partially to comply with wage increases negotiated in 1981, the union rejected the move. The union protested by refusing overtime and announced, "If they want war, they'll have it." The rhetoric of violence increased considerably in 1984. Union leaders feared that the sale of the plot of land by the company might be part of a plan to close down Metal Empresa. Among the other violent slogans that appeared in the union newspaper, the union pronounced, "Our rights will not be mortgaged, they will be defended with blood."

At the same time, conflicts were exacerbated by the extreme combativeness of actions and violent threats from the union. In 1981, three workers were thrown out of the union for failing to comply with the obligatory work rotations outside of Lima. Notwithstanding their expulsion from the union, company officials allowed the workers to enter the union-controlled cafeteria. This provoked an impromptu union meeting during work hours. The union charged "employer harassment." In response to an announcement that the company would suspend the normal Sunday pay in light of the work stoppage, the union declared that it would not permit the sanction, with the threat that "blood will flow."

Between 1980 and 1984, the union took over the plant three times. On 30 April 1981, the union took over the plant for the first time when the company failed to pay the week's wages. The union did not believe the company's explanations that it could not meet the payroll because of problems with the banks. "We know their tricks," leaders wrote in the union newspaper. On 26 and 27 July 1983, the workers' union together with the office workers took over the plant when the company failed to pay wages, salaries, and midyear bonuses. This took place despite the fact that the newly inaugurated union leaders had editorialized that they would "not fall into dogmatism by using recipes or slogans that had been effective in the past." Finally, the union took over the plant again on 12 April 1984. The takeover was the result of several problems. In the first place, the union protested the company's decision to split the benefit payments of twelve thousand soles that workers received at the start of the school year into two parts: one part was to be paid initially, the remainder at the end of the month. One day before this, the company docked the pay of workers who were protesting the company's failure to provide transportation expenses for their travel to work sites at the port. The union insisted that the company hand over the docked pay of the twelve workers, pay the travel expenses they demanded, and disburse the school benefits in a single payment. During discussions about the first point, company officials withdrew from the meeting to consult among themselves. At that point, leaders broke off the negotiations and went to the factory doors to lock them up with chains. They did so without consulting with the rank-and-file workers. The takeover was lifted a few hours later by union leaders without producing any results and cost two union leaders their jobs.

The union reacted to the cuts in benefits and disregard for workers' rights with greater and greater hostility. That hostility, however, remained contained within the firm. Even as frustration and mistrust produced impulsive and sporadic acts of violence in response to specific circumstances, the union did not find a way to coordinate collective action with workers outside of Metal Empresa. The traditional solidarity expressed in federation-backed, industry-wide strikes broke down. In March 1980, the Metal Empresa union agreed not to join a strike of the Federación de Trabajadores de la Industria Metalúrgica. The union had been one of the most renowned affiliates of the Federación. The leftist activists who had incorporated workers in the Federación and political activities disengaged from such organizing. Workers resented it: "Hugo Blanco and Javier Diez Canseco have come here," one Metal Empresa worker complained, "they have been elected by us and now where are they? Nobody knows."[1]

The increase in the use of violent tactics by the union, however, did not reflect rising passions on the part of the rank and file. While leaders became increasingly violent in their interactions with the company, workers endorsed union extremism only in a passive, conformist way. In February 1984, the leaders complained in the union newspaper that the workers expected that "the leaders alone win their battle." They pointed out that "the majority of workers are greatly to blame because they attend assemblies like they were tourists, expressing conformity in the face of the company's rhetoric." As a former union leader said, "People are demoralized; they are told one thing and they say fine; then are told something else and they say that's okay too." That passivity was evident, for example, during the last plant takeover in April 1984: the workers backed the takeover decreed by the leaders without consulting with them while they were at work in the factory, just as they backed the lifting of it without any opposition.

The lack of conviction that workers felt vis-à-vis union extremism in the factory, combined with the lack of clear political views, made for a situation in which workers felt impotent. The feeling was described by the former union leader Jorge Villón in the following terms: "If we fight, we're screwed, if we don't fight, we're still screwed." Under these circumstances, the social and political identity of the workers that was born in the 1970s persisted as a kind of passive clasismo. Working-class consciousness revolved around resentment, rage, and blaming the powerful. For Eugenio Vilcapoma, for example, all those politicians, company owners, and officials "who didn't even pay attention to the smallest thing that was happening to people" were to blame for the situation. As he put it, "The government is to blame, followed by the big businessmen, who are followed by the senators, representatives, and cabinet ministers. Wages are of no interest to them." To Vilcapoma, even prices were part of a strategy of class-based segregation. This was his interpretation of the increase in the cost of school supplies: "The big businessmen thought: if they're all going to study, all are really going to get smart. Even the intelligentsia isn't going to dominate as easily as they do now. Today we're seeing it, with the little experience, with the little knowledge that we have, we're not going to allow ourselves to be violated as we did when we used to work for twelve hours a day."

PART II

In His Own Words
The Many Lives of Jesús Zúñiga

7
Childhood
We'd Be Winners Someday

I am Jesús Zúñiga Sotomayor, a native of the Curpahuasi district, from the province of Grau, in the department of Apurímac.

My father had a good bit of land, so did my mother. My mother was the daughter of the local mayor, whose name was Sotomayor. They were landowners. But what can you do with so much land when there's no seed or rain, and the people begin to get scared if it doesn't rain because there's nothing to eat, only what is stored from one year to the next? People around there mainly harvest to eat, not to sell. They barter and exchange. Those who don't have any corn swap for potatoes, and those who don't have any potatoes do the same.

The land is worked in a communal fashion. When I was five years old I helped by carrying firewood or grass and herding livestock when there was some.

As far as I can remember, I left the farm when I was about six years old with my father, Wenceslao Zúñiga Vargas, who went to work as a miner in Cuchachaina, a mine located in the town of Progreso, facing Curpahuasi. At that age, I hadn't yet been to the district school. The school only went up to the third grade and it was a single room in which everyone studied. Those in higher grades faced one side and those from all the grades of primary school faced in the opposite direction, in other words, with their backs to each other.

When the Cuchachaina mine closed, I went back with my father to Curpahuasi, where my mother and two sisters were. I didn't get along with my mom. I'm not saying that she punished me; she worried about me when she saw that I wasn't as close to her as my sisters were. But I had always been more attached to my old man. I liked his dynamism a lot, and he was very helpful. He had spent time in Arequipa before and had learned Spanish quickly. He was one of the few who spoke it in my town. Once we went to Cuzco and all of a sudden he decided to carry suitcases for passengers at the airport. He'd go around with a rope tied to his body and loaded down with suitcases. I'd help him by collecting for the service.

My father didn't like farmwork very much. Upon return to Cuchachaina, he went to Limatambo, in Cuzco, to work as a shopkeeper. I couldn't get accustomed to staying behind in my hometown. I wanted to go with my father. When he returned five months later, I wouldn't let the old man go again and he took me with him to his job in the Condor Mine, located near Pisco. Then he was transferred to the San Juan Mine of Lucanas, in Uti, where we worked for nearly four years. My dad liked being a miner. He was a driller and preferred to work with contractors, working twelve hours a day for higher wages. He did his work without any protective gear at all. So, I think that the mine killed him because after Uti he worked in other mines. Then he died when he was around fifty years old.

When we were in the mine at Uti, I used to work in Señora Graciela's restaurant, where they served breakfast, lunch, and dinner to more than two hundred miners. There were about fifteen boys and girls mostly from Cuzco, Puno, Apurímac, and Ayacucho. We all worked. Pointing to me when I helped my dad, the lady used to say to her own children, "Look how hard this boy works." Without my asking him to, my father always brought her firewood or water. In gratitude, she didn't charge us for food. At night, I began to go to school and I learned to read. I read the news from the newspaper to my father when he got home. He was illiterate and he only knew how to sign his name. My father would become emotional when I read and he'd hug me and cry.

On account of my work at the restaurant, I regularly traveled to fetch fruits and vegetables. We used to go to Puquio, Nazca, and Ica. We'd go to Lima but only as far as Parada. During the truck ride in the city, I'd look on all sides to see if I saw my sister Alejandra, who had come to Lima to work in Sotomayor's hat factory. The factory belonged to a brother of my mom's father. I had no idea how big the city was, but I was becoming familiar with the atmosphere.

When I was ten years old, my father left me to go work at the Acarí Mine. He signed a contract with Señora Graciela and with Señor Tapia. It specified that I'd stay to work with them. Once my sister Alejandra came to take me to Lima, but I refused to go. I was happy there since there were many boys like me who worked and studied half a day. Besides, we all were very much liked by all the workers. They had always praised us, saying that someday we'd be at the top of the heap, that we'd be winners someday. That was because we could work from four in the morning on, first to prepare breakfasts, and we ended our chores at eleven or twelve at night by washing the pots, dishes, and all the silverware so as to leave the dining room, kitchen, and everything that was needed clean for the next day. I ended up staying in Uti for a long time, more or less until the age of eleven or twelve.

Afterward, I went back to the farm and was there some four or five months. But I could not get used to it because what I wanted to do by then was work. I couldn't get accustomed to my mother or my sisters. I just wanted to be left alone. Then my father decided to go with me again to the Condor Mine, which is in Pisco. We were around there for about five or six months until we came to Lima.

8

Lima
The Light Seemed Like Daylight

When I arrived in Lima, I stayed at my Uncle Marcos's house. He was my father's brother. His house was on Avenida Argentina. My father returned from the mountains and he stayed with me, starting to work in an insecticides business.

I began to work in the Grillón, at a food stand that was on Avenida Argentina near my uncle's house. The workers from the nearby factory would eat there. The owner was a hardworking old man who got up at four in the morning and went to bed at eleven at night. He ended up owning three houses and at each one he raised chickens and pigs. The stand is still on Faucett Avenue in a spot that some Italians gave to the old man.

I used to study at night. I was in the second grade of primary school. I was more advanced than the others. The teacher, a person from Huancayo like me, became my friend. He'd always ask for students to go up in front of the class to speak and he'd ask for volunteers. People would chicken out. Then he'd say that there weren't any men tough enough to get up and talk. So then I'd get up and would speak a little bit and that was that. My classmates would congratulate me and the teacher would too. Then the teacher made a deal for me to skip a grade and pass in a year and a half from second to third grade of primary school.

I worked at the food stand for two years. Then I was hospitalized in the Carrión Hospital for nearly a year and a half because my knees were crooked. As the doctor explained, they were crooked from all the weight I put on them in the mine. Or maybe it was because Señora Graciela raised pigs and we carried pails of food to them, but my legs weren't strong enough and with the weight they got crooked. Day by day my legs were getting more deformed because they were skinny. Anyway, I was in unbearable pain. Because of that, I decided to go to Carrión Hospital, where they admitted me. They operated on me there. I had a cast from my chest down to my legs for a year. I could be lifted or stand up only with help.

For me, someone who had always been active and restless, it was very hard to accept. I was very well liked in the hospital. Everyone admired me: nurses, doctors, patients, and patients' relatives. I helped make the beds. I changed clothes. I took care of the hospitalized children. I got the bedpan for them. The patients' relatives, especially the children's, used to bring me fruits. My sister Alejandra visited me on Sundays.

When I got better they let me out and my cousins took me to Rímac Beach to sunbathe. So that, little by little, I felt better until one day I took the cast off by myself. I refused to go back to the hospital anymore. I sold pastries on a tricycle to the workers at Bata-Rímac, Copsa, and other companies.

I've always liked soccer. When I was about sixteen years old, I went for the first time to the national stadium to a game played at night. This time, two doctors who had taken a liking to me when I was in Carrión Hospital took me to the game. I didn't understand how they could play on a field at night. I had never seen so many people gathered together. The lights seemed like daylight, and it amazed me.

9

Everything Was Great
When I Started at the Factory

One day my father fought with my uncle and they threw us out. We had to go to my Uncle Celestino's house. He was one of my mother's brothers who used to live in what is now known as Pueblo Joven Planeta, at the top of the twelfth block of Avenida Argentina. In time, I fought with my uncle. This time, they only threw me out. I had to rent a single room around Ecuador Street in the same area. Then I went to work in a brickyard that was located in Conde de Vega, now called Pueblo Joven Rescate, bordering Planeta.

I started at the bottom in the brickyard, doing the toughest jobs like carrying the guano that they lined the kiln with. We even worked on Saturdays and Sundays, but later on, we got good pay.

At the age of about sixteen and a half, I got into working construction on Avenida Brasil. It was a very tough job. I was in construction work for about two years. I left that job on the advice that my brother-in-law gave me. He told me that there was not much to learn in construction; that the job was very tough and that even though I might be earning seventy soles a day, money wasn't everything in life. It would be better for me to get into the metallurgical industry because it was a better place to work and learn. My brother-in-law was a supervisor in Promecán, and he told me that I could learn boilermaking, welding, and reading blueprints and that I could study at night. All this could be useful to me later on.

I paid attention to him, since my sister was also whining a lot about the fact that I was working in construction. She was afraid that my knee problems might get worse and she spoke to her husband. So I took the job he got for me and I quit construction work. He spoke with the personnel manager and the engineer and they took me in. In construction, I was earning seventy soles. When I went into Promecán, I was making forty soles.

I joined Promecán as a blowtorch assistant. The job impressed me a lot: cutting the steel sheets and welding. My first tasks included getting the hoses—where the oxygen goes through one end and the oil through the other—cleaning the sheets and the work area, throwing water on the floor or on the sheet metal, and holding the straight edge to do the tracing. The senior workman didn't teach me much. He was somewhat selfish, but above all he was quiet. He hardly talked and would only speak to say, "Grab here, get over there," and so on. Almost all of the senior workmen were this way. You had to take them gifts, detergent, soap, so that they might teach you something. Then they rotated me to work with the drill punch operators, at the request of my brother-in-law. I was with the senior workman, José Alcántara, who taught me to use the pressure gauge that controls the outflow of the oxygen and the acetylene from the blowtorch. With the senior workman, named Gavidia, we followed a routine. It was like this: first, get the job production order; second, get the order from the supervisor with a blueprint of the job and the authorization for removing material from the warehouse; third, bring the material; fourth, trace the sheet metal according to specifications; fifth, cut and bevel; and finally, hand over the work. That's what I did.

There was plenty of work. There were 1,600 workers and some 250 engineers. It was a huge number of workers. It got my attention seeing so many people and so many boilermakers, the boats, and the barges. Everything was great when I started working there. Also, I liked the meetings a lot which the people held at the gates. The union leaders got on the top of buses and led the meetings from there. I've always liked that kind of meeting. I think that is the reason why I hung around and was among the last thirty-five or forty persons that kept going to the meetings before the company closed down. I didn't know what a union was, it was like an adventure just to see what was going on.

Once Promecán closed, the union leaders were blamed because they were pushing a list of demands. It was said that they closed down the company because of the factory takeovers done by metallurgical workers in 1964. That's the kind of thing that was said. That's even what the former Promecán workers who now work at Metal Empresa believe. But I think the closure was because of a political decision by the owners and stockholders, because when Promecán went broke, it went bankrupt with a large amount of work left to be done. When Metal Empresa opened, they kept on building the ships that Promecán had left unfinished. I think the closing had to do with a political calculation by the partners and the Belaúnde government. And on the other hand, I think there was also a lack of direction in organizing the union.

10
Hard Workers and Shirkers

When I started at Metal Empresa, we used to pay for our work clothes and shoes. There was no cafeteria. We used to have lunch on the street corner as if we were nobodies. There was transportation only up to Plaza Unión and to the Callao Obelisk. To other parts of the city, there wasn't any. We used to be watched a lot. You had to be at work at 7:30, and there were no excuses allowed for tardiness even though most workers lived in *pueblos jovenes* like Villa El Salvador, Comas, Collique, or Cantogrande. In the mornings, it was tough to get there on time.

The treatment by the engineers and the personnel manager was very abusive and overbearing. You couldn't even answer or talk back because they'd toss you out on the street right then and there. You worked under a three- or six-month contract so that you had to grin and bear it. Besides, for the group of blowtorch specialists, welders, boilermakers, and machine operators, who were most of those employed in the metallurgical industry, there wasn't any work at that time, so people put up with it.

At the time, there was a group of talareños who were buddies of the personnel manager. He had his people who were sort of thugs, streetwise as they say, and tough, who had privileges. They wouldn't go to work on Mondays. But their time cards would appear punched and they'd get paid for the full week. They'd get permission to leave work for an emergency. These were the kind of privileges they had. They'd arrive late and they'd just let them into work. If they needed to go to medical appointments and had permission, they wouldn't deduct the extra Sunday pay or any other hours. In contrast, for anybody else, they took it out of your pay. I think that kind of thing going on created the conditions that made the workers and compañeros wake up and see that it was necessary to organize themselves and form a union.

Most of the people from the sierra were dedicated to their work. They were a people who got a lot of respect from the *chalacos* [people from Callao, the port adjacent to Lima] and the limeños because they were polite and hardworking. Even the engineers and the bosses clearly saw that those people stood out the most because of their productivity on the job.

The people from the sierra don't chicken out when they face problems. In that sense, it's said of the serrano that even if he has to go uphill to feed the pigs he'll do it. You can point to how people have built their homes on the hills of San Cosme, in Comas, and in areas like these, and how people have been able to carry up bricks, cement, water, and stones to be able to build their homes. In that sense, the provincial people, especially the serranos, are often illiterate but there's something in their nature that shines through and that's that they don't chicken out; they go on ahead and confront problems as they come up. I think that's true as much in business as at work, and they don't cheat, unlike the limeños as far as I've gotten to know them. In the brickyard where I used to work, the limeños wouldn't go where the bricks were loaded. Whenever you take a brick out of the kiln, it is thrown down to a loading dock where a worker has to catch it and you can get hit by the brick. The limeños didn't stay around there but rather went up on the platform.

In the same way, they always tried to hide themselves in the factory someplace because they were wise guys while the person who did go in to work was the serrano. The limeño is a shirker, that is, they play dumb, they crawl into boxes to sleep or do these kinds of things. For example, if we're going to carry a table among several persons, the limeño acts like he's holding up his end but doesn't use any of his strength—or he's looking for something to protect his hands. He's lazy because of his environment. The limeño hasn't gotten up at three in the morning to herd cattle or carry firewood.

They always have thought of themselves as the bright ones, as unlike the serranos, who are very hardworking and talented. I've been able to see that in my section, especially. When we were a section, you might say that we were the motor of the plant. We were the engine of the plant, so to speak, since that's where the main machines for cutting and customizing were and everyone was very honest and hardworking and there were even two or three talareños who were also very good people. Also, there were two chalacos who, little by little, have completely changed from what they used to be like and have been really influenced for the better by us. We were a very close-knit section, even though the union organization didn't exist yet.

11

The Union

We Were No Longer What We Were Before

The difference between criollos and serranos in the factory was changing over time, especially as a result of the union organization. Respect for co-workers and leaders and a sense of solidarity take hold when a union exists. The criollos realized that no matter how brave they might be, by themselves they were definitely isolated. I saw that they were coming to understand that mutual support was in everybody's interest, not just for us in our section, but for the entire rank and file. As far as I could tell, they started changing their attitude once the union organization, in conjunction with the workers, began to win a series of general benefits that hadn't existed before there was a union. Changes on the job, in the trades, in productivity, in taking on the tasks of union organizing, the presence of the workers themselves in the union meetings — everything was changing. For me, it was a fascinating change. I think that it has been the most important learning experience, not only for them [workers] but also for their families. Because we were no longer what we were before.

Getting a cafeteria and winning work shoes and a uniform was a very important thing. That kind of thing benefited everybody, and it was won by the union with the workers behind it. Of course there were a few workers who wanted to back off, but the compañeros themselves imposed discipline and I think everyone came to accept this.

But the most important victory for me has been the matter of family leave benefits. This was an issue that affected me when my wife gave birth. Because I didn't have 750 soles on hand, I couldn't get my son out of the maternity ward. I had to borrow it from some compañeros. This happened when there still wasn't a union. This concession was won along with other important benefits, almost twenty-eight of all the bargaining points were won, but this one was what got my attention most. First, because the average worker doesn't have domestic help and this was one argument that put the company's bargaining committee in a corner. We said to them,

"What do you do if they call you on the phone and tell you your wife is having her labor pains?" A worker doesn't even have a telephone, or any way to communicate with his wife, or a chance to call her a taxi, or any way to contact her, or maybe go take care of her. Those were some of the arguments made so that the company had no choice but to accept. Besides, we told them that a worker takes a leave only to take care of his wife and to get the baby's birth certificate registered. These responsibilities should not result in a worker losing his Sunday or daily wage (these are vital necessities, not a luxury, in household finances). I think that this was a political issue, and I've always maintained this position. There are now two days of family leave and it's the worker's call, he can ask for it if he wants, either both days consecutively or he can request a number of hours until he gets to complete a full two days of time. This has been a very valuable benefit for the workers, especially for their wives, who have often expressed their gratitude.

Another of the concessions, which I can also highlight, is leave time for union activity. Many other strong federations and powerful unions here in Peru haven't managed to get what the workers' union of Metal Empresa achieved. This is open, unscheduled leave time for union leaders, of which there are six. This has benefited the rank and file a lot, and this benefit has been won by other unions and has created ties to neighborhood and popular organizations. That's because we, the leaders, have had the privilege or the luck, thanks to this victory, of being able to converse with people from other organizations, both above and below. But ultimately, especially for me, it was a learning experience, a great learning opportunity to attend mass events and to be present in the name of the rank and file at political rallies. Many times I was the main speaker in short union courses, in founding day celebrations of pueblos jovenes, and in the universities. In this way I made very important contacts. It was an especially valuable learning experience, and I came fully to understand the significance of this as a bargaining concession. And thanks to that experience, we have been able to spread the word to other unions like the Quesada factory, where flexible leave for their union leaders was also won.

Another equally valuable concession which, especially for me, meant the joy of seeing our workers getting together was a holiday for the workers on 17 October. This is the day we triumphed in organizing the union, the anniversary of our union. Union leaders rightly emphasize its importance. We have always celebrated this together with the workers' wives, their children, and all their families. I remember that on one occasion we managed to have all the children, under the direction of a committee, get on the ships and go up to the boilers so they could see how they're welded, how the metal is cut, and see the blueprints. For the little kids, it was a tremendous novelty. It was also exciting for workers' wives who never had seen where their husband or boyfriend worked. For sisters as well and even workers' mothers, it was a great occasion, and many cried. We threw a magnificent party to celebrate the first year that this concession was won. I think even now the compañeros continue celebrating this like a birthday with all their families.

But apart from that, we had the Secretaría de Asistencia Social (Secretariat of Social Assistance). I have always maintained that the Secretaría de Asistencia Social is the heart of the union. It's the Secretaría that's always there, making union solidarity a reality with help especially when a worker or comrade is sick or when some relative finds himself in some difficulty. The secretary for social assistance has always been a person in whom we, the leaders, placed our complete trust because he would have to go to any place where he was needed and he had decision-making powers. We'd take up contributions for the death of a brother, mother, child, or wife. All the workers contributed so that the Secretaría could extend the help we gave. That was a contribution from all of us. It was not only for the factory workers but whenever other unions were on strike or they came and asked us for help, it was given to them and we didn't mind. I think that in this way the Metal Empresa workers were quite progressive.

12

Deceived by the Company, but Hopeful in the Struggle

The most important moment for the union was the first year when it presented its list of demands. People had great expectations that the company would concede to the list of demands rapidly because business was good. Some of us used to work up to three shifts. So there was an expectation among all of us that the company would quickly give in to the list of demands in order to go on working.

But this wasn't the case. I think the company came down on us hard after the first list of demands, which provoked a fourteen-day strike to obtain only a fifteen-soles raise. Many of us got to know each other in the course of working on that strike and going to ask other unions for contributions. In that strike only three or four workers betrayed us, or in other words, made a mistake, which they made up for in the end. They recognized that they had made a mistake and later some even took positions as section delegates.

But that strike was a very important learning experience for the rank and file because they came to know the quality of the leaders that they had up front. The leaders also saw that, even with all the internal problems, support existed in the rank and file and there was honesty. It showed because when the second resolution, the definitive one, came from the Ministry of Labor, giving us a raise of fifteen soles, a lot of people in the assembly even cried and said that they'd strike for one more day for free, just to make a point. That decision, in my view, was very important because far from being frightened in that strike, people went back to work feeling strengthened. Everyone was aware that, thanks to that form of struggle, the strike, they had won a victory of fifteen soles when the company wouldn't have offered us absolutely anything. Because of this, the internal organization took off. The assemblies started and delegates were organized for every section in the plant. It was a very intense job and I think people became more aware. Because of this, they always saw the strike as a way out of any problem. As a means of showing strength, the strike always produced good results. Many times, people even overruled the leaders because they saw the strike as a solution for everything. The company pretended to be poor and it wouldn't give in. But the same basic needs brought the people together until there was a solid unity. Thanks to that unity, proposals were developed by leaders and delegates together. And after discussion at the assembly, they presented them to the company. But the company pretended that it didn't have enough money and that it couldn't meet the demands.

On one occasion, a study was done of the company's economic situation. All the union members contributed some money to do this study, but the study showed the company registering losses. So everyone discounted the study. Legally speaking, the company was working at a loss, and we gave up on the idea of getting at the profits through the Industrial Community. Instead, our idea was to win some benefits through the union. The account balances appeared low, and the documents that we managed to obtain made us think that they were made up, but there wasn't any way to prove it. People then lost interest.

We believed that the company didn't have losses because of what the consultants had told us after conducting a review of the accounts. With the boom in the metallurgical industry, I figured that the company was earning a 60 or 50 percent profit. I calculated that based on what I'd seen at other places, like for example Pisca, which shared its profits with its workers. It seems that the company's trick was to borrow money from another company, which was its main stockholder, and then it had to pay them back like the government does with the International Monetary Fund. We knew that the company was producing and therefore our only option was to get benefits through the union. Rather than push for our 100,000 or 150,000 soles which they might have given us in profit sharing, we sought concessions like the ones we had already obtained.

13

Jesús and Politics

Ever since the union was founded, I knew that Vanguardia Revolucionaria, a political party, was on the scene. During the first strike, VR members were there, getting up with us to be on the picket line early and hand-
ing out their flyers of support. There was a big guy who they called Panzer,
who was always there. To speak, he got up on a bench. And it was even
more impressive when they spoke from on top of parked cars. All of that
impressed me. Once a delegation came from the Cuban government because it was interested in ordering some boats built and the union put up
a huge red banner which said: "Welcome Cuban Compañeros. Long live
the Cuban Revolution."

The students went to the factories because they wanted to ally themselves with workers. Whether it might be in organizing unions or helping
in a series of tasks like making up flyers during a strike, distributing them,
asking for contributions in the markets or factories, and organizing working committees (which in many cases the workers didn't understand), the
students did it. The students knew a lot of political theory, but they were
anxious to put their ideas into practice. I saw that was the job they had
to do. Apart from that, their main goal was to attract people to the organization, the political party. For them, it had to do with signing up new
members, seeing what people they had to talk to in order to get them to
join the party. Their main goal was chiefly to be in contact with the union
leaders.

I saw that the union leaders worked hard, they went all over the place.
There was Quiroz, "El Chino" Salazar, and in the assemblies, Chuquija,
who was from Puno, Ninahuanca from Ancash, and myself. We were all
young guys. We always defended our leadership especially against the old
men who would call us "irresponsible boys." Then they spoke to me about
joining a political group and I accepted. As far as I can recall, in those days
Vanguardia Revolucionaria was the organization that would go out into

the streets in places such as Plaza Unión, Dos de Mayo, Manco Cápac, and Avenida Abancay. The National Library was one of the key spots where a group of us—say, twenty, thirty, fifteen, or ten of us—gave speeches. I think that was my defining experience in Vanguardia. On the other hand, at that time, publications about peasant leaders were coming out in which Lino Quintanilla, may he rest in peace, as well as Andrés Luna Vargas, were mentioned a lot. At that time, I didn't know what they were like but I was very interested in knowing them. All these things influenced me to join Vanguardia. Above all, the determining factor was that I belonged to the Metal Empresa union.

Once they invited me to a talk at the party headquarters. We went there with Quiroz, Salazar, and compañeros from other places. Recognizing him by his name tag, they introduced themselves to the speaker, who was Ricardo Letts.[1] I knew about him because his speeches appeared in the newspapers. His presence impressed me a lot. He shook my hand. His hand was very big, and he said to me, "How are you, compañero?" He had just arrived from Cuba and spoke about that in his talk. He told us that we the workers should organize ourselves to serve our people. By the end, I felt a greater commitment. It was definitive.

In the party, my relationship with the leaders has been practically non-existent. I always heard them speak about *"Chato"* [Shorty] and that there were three or four compañeros assigned in La Oroya to organize the miners. Others were organizing the sugarcane cutters of the North and so on. But there wasn't any continuing relationship with them [the leaders], let's say, except through documents, reports that were produced inside the organization about the decisions made and the tasks they had to accomplish.

I met party leader Edmundo Murrugarra in University Park.[2] It was a last-minute rally called by the party and it had been decided that he should speak. When the police came, I beat it out of there, running with several male and female compañeros. By the time I got to Grau Street, I had met up with some compañeros who knew me and surrounded me and introduced me to Compañero Murrugarra. Then we went to a meeting to do an evaluation of the event, of the march, and of the last-minute rally that took place. Thus I had an opportunity to meet Edmundo Murrugarra. He told me two or three things. Just as Letts had impressed me, he impressed me just as much, especially because of his simplicity. He offered me some words of encouragement and from then on we got together a little more frequently; by that time, it had been decided that I had to be a publicly known union leader because of the things the party had determined.

One thing that made me feel uncomfortable about the party was that it didn't appreciate the effort or the sacrifice you made for the organization. As workers, we had to live up to our obligations in the factory, especially the shift schedules for coming and going. There you didn't hesitate to fulfill your responsibility like any person or worker did. You got out at five or six in the afternoon and from there you had to attend a meeting. It was often very far away; in many cases, you couldn't count on having enough for the bus fare, but it was your responsibility and obligation to attend; and the meeting went on until the late hours of the night and naturally this was something of a bother. In other words, in my view, all the efforts made by so many people were never taken into account. I think, for that reason, many people dropped out. It was not because of a lack of goodwill or commitment, but unfortunately, here in Lima, you need money. If there isn't any, it's difficult then for you to live and especially if you have a wife and children. In my view, that hasn't been taken into account. Apart from everything else, you had to put in your required dues for the organization and at the same time finance the party newspaper with whatever you could. But it was an obligation and we all lived up to it.

In 1972, the union organized a brief union course. I was the sports delegate from my section and I attended the brief course. It helped me a lot. I learned things that I didn't know like the history of the workers' movement and other things like that. Then in 1973, I was elected secretary general of the union without having held another union office before. We demanded wage increases and better working conditions from the employer. The only way to obtain those things was through the union. First, we sized up the company. If the company refused, as it always did, the only alternative was getting together and taking forceful measures. At the time, we had an internal policy of consulting with people about going after those wage benefits and improved working conditions. But also it was explained to people that coming together through union organizations would make it possible to bring together workers from different workplaces. Now that meant thinking about something else, a political party, which would help us hook up with the peasants and other social sectors who are our allies and put forth a list of demands to the government.

Things were governed, in my view, by politics. In other words, education, health, job security, or whatever it might be, all were regulated by politics. But workers have always been left out of politics. In other words, workers are just plain workers for eight or twelve hours a day. Therefore, whenever I've gotten involved, I've stressed that it's necessary to play politics. For example, I consider that getting two days of leave in order to be present at the labor and delivery of your wife was a very special, politically significant concession. Getting it meant overcoming all the obstacles that existed and getting a break for working people, especially for wives and for the child who is born crying and doesn't know how to do anything else. From my standpoint, then and now, the most important thing that the Peruvian people have is their children. Today, many people are worried about children as seen in the Fundación por los Niños, the Vaso de Leche, day care centers, and soup kitchens. I think that this was a very special concession politically because the issue had, up until that time, seemed nonexistent. When people began to benefit from that concession, they discovered its value.

In that sense, one of the responsibilities which we as activists have to assume because of the influence we had on unions was failing to foresee wage depreciation. This was the central issue which all the country's organizations, especially the Left, had neglected to deal with. This was especially the case with Vanguardia, which in many cases had taken the initiative in foreseeing and warning against attacks and making concrete proposals at the union and Federación levels. But in this case, I think we were careless, and also we neglected to provide a very concrete and well-defined response to the massive firing of union leaders after 19 July 1977. I think all the leftist political parties and especially the Communist Party were responsible for allowing the loss of an entire group of leaders. It was a huge investment on the part of people to educate such an excellent and extraordinary group of leaders, and all of this was wasted. A political response couldn't be made in the face of the political measures of the Morales Bermúdez dictatorship. I think that has been one of the greatest betrayals of the PC [Communist Party] "Unity" and of all the leftist parties. It will be a long time before another grassroots movement of our people will emerge with those characteristics and the level of consciousness those people had at that time. No political party has been able to organize those groups of people which today we often see begging, many are ill with tuberculosis, and there are many others who don't even have money for medicine. I am familiar with many cases and it truly pains me, but it remains something that is hard to talk about. It's like a thorn stuck in my side. But I understand that that's the way it will feel and how it ought to feel when you're committed to sacrificing and really giving your all to our people; not just you alone, but with your entire family.

I believe that the effort of these people, of the compañeros, serves as an example, especially for the union organizations, which keep going and should keep going. It's the same for the squatters' land invasions that have been carried out in Lima, which above all should be kept in the hearts of everyone in the factories. As I forcefully put it to my fellow Peruvians: "Yes, damn it, the so-called serrano trash has taken over Lima, hell! We'll see how far we can go!" We're going to show that this is the true Peruvian people, and I think that the country is with us. I believe that nobody is going to put up with crap; they're not going to take it anymore. In Lima, the serranos, the provincial people from the North, South, East, and West, are going to show what they are capable of doing and that they're capable of saying, "Damn it! We're the real Peruvians!" I think that our country is moving toward showing its true identity and not hiding what the Peruvian people are, with all their problems, their misery, their hunger, because all this is the product of the sellouts of every government that has led our people for more than 450 years. Because of that, we have always been trampled underfoot: our grandfathers, great-grandfathers, and our fathers, but I think that today, people from the provinces have begun to develop a consciousness.

14

If This Turns Out Okay,
to Hell with the Company

When I started at Metal Empresa, my ambition was to be a great businessman. But in the company, I was devoted to the union and the plans I
had went down the tubes. Anyway, while I was a leader, I couldn't work
overtime in the factory, but I needed more income because I was taking
care of my brothers. Among the workers, I sold combs, handkerchiefs,
and ballpoint pens. Afterward, I set up a food stand to sell breakfasts in
front of the plant. I also set up a beer warehouse with Ramón Espinoza,
but it didn't turn out well.

In 1975, I set up a chicken farm with Salazar. Salazar had bought a plot
of land. With seven thousand soles we bought all the stakes and mats
and at night, after work, we made the chicken coops. Later, with our July
bonus, we bought six thousand chicks, which arrived in little boxes, and
we put a thousand chickens in each coop. While the chicks were still tiny,
we got an offer to sell them and it was a good deal for us. But we began
to think, If this is what they're offering us now, how much more might
they offer us when the chicks are fully grown? So we didn't sell them,
but it turns out that you have to give a lot of feed to chicks and we were
running out of money. Then we began to borrow from everybody. We
hit on everyone, even for the smallest sums, until we no longer had any
place to go for a loan. A few days went by and the chicks didn't have any
feed left when happily a few compañeros, who had gotten a loan from the
company, gave us the money. With that, we could finish fattening up the
chicks. But as it turned out, when we tried to sell them, there wasn't anybody to buy them. Also as time went by, again we didn't have any feed.
Then we decided to go out and sell them ourselves. We put some chickens
in sacks and went one Sunday to Acho to sell them. It was very sunny and
we weren't selling many and after a few hours the chickens started smell-
ing bad. Somebody said to us, "Why don't you just give them away to the

ladies from the neighborhood and get rid of them?" We went back to the farm and we didn't know what to do. Over the next few days, we went directly to the markets of Callao and they began to move until we sold all of them. When we finished, we had earned a profit. Then we paid all our debts and we improved the chicken coops by putting in floors and lights. With the experience we had, we thought that indeed this was going to turn out well. Chino [Salazar] said: "Look, if this turns out okay, to hell with the company, I'm quitting! Then you leave too and we'll make a fortune. We're killing ourselves for such assholes, why can't we just bust our butts for ourselves?" We bought six thousand chicks again and when we sold them, we made more money. Then Chino got a pickup truck for himself by making a down payment, for the purpose of delivering the chickens. But the third round turned out badly for us because the prices dropped and we lost money.

On another occasion, they let me in on forming a group with Valverde, Pacheco, Licona, and Peralta to set up a metal repair workshop. We were all workers with on-the-job experience and the idea was to quit and, with our severance pay, set up the business. But in the end, almost all chickened out and they didn't leave the factory.

On another occasion, I bought two dollies at forty thousand soles and I sold them for one hundred forty thousand. Then with Quiroz and Peralta, we bought a batch of stoves and we sold them. From there I proposed buying a batch of scrap metal which Metal Empresa was selling. We submitted our letter with an offer of eighty cents per kilo but another person actually beat us out with a lower bid.

Then Peralta said to me, "I can't go on here, I have six kids and we're never going to get ahead." Then, out of that, another idea for a workshop was born. The idea was to get out of the factory and, with our severance pay, set up a shop. I said to him: "Look, Flaco [Peralta], since I'm a union leader, I can't quit. The one who has to quit is you." Then Flaco set out on his own. This was in 1976.

Afterward in 1977, I set up a restaurant in Rímac which my brother was managing, but it went broke. Also with Peralta, we bought a used truck from a workshop, paying for it with a sixty thousand soles bank loan. I knew the engineer who was the owner of the workshop, and he put a lot of trust in me. We used the truck for deliveries of iron and cement, and we contracted a driver who was living in Peralta's house and in exchange we gave him free rent.

15
Breaking Bread

I had the good fortune of being committed to a woman who I love and with whom I've had two children, a little girl and a boy. As luck would have it, it was just at the time when I was giving 90 percent of my time to the party, union organizing and the neighborhood struggle.

I already knew her, and one day we went out to the beach on a whim. It was in September 1970. I remember that there was a rally at the Palacio de Gobierno with Velasco and we went because we were curious to hear El Chino (popular nickname for General Velasco). Well, after that, we began to live together.

The day when we got married, I invited the Asians who came to Metal Empresa as technical advisers from Japan and two of them came. It was a very simple gathering. Some provincial friends attended, Delmer Quiroz, and nobody else.

We started out in a little room that I had on Ecuador Street in front of the Eternit factory. Since there wasn't running water or anything, I went ahead and leased an apartment on Avenida Argentina when my son was born. A co-worker had leased it to me, so my wife went there with my son directly from the maternity ward. Later, I tried to build a house in Canto Grande but it didn't work out, so I'm still where I began. As time goes on, we're going to see what possibilities there might be for moving.

I often remember Dr. Laura Caller, who gave a small seminar for a few people about the need to not have more children. Just then, I already had my son, and my wife was pregnant again. Well, my compañera and I came to the conclusion that it was very important for me and for her not to have any more kids. We ended up with two children. My son Pepe was born on 13 July 1972 and my daughter on 31 July 1973. In other words, in a single year we had two kids, the two that I have now.

As in every home, I know that there has been hunger and misery in my house. But I think the greatest part for me has been being with my wife, my compañera, and my two children. I have gone through some very tough times but, thanks to my spouse, we stay together. Like any mother, although there may not be any bread in the house, she gives my two children the kisses that sustain them. I think that's what fills the bellies of babies.

During the years I was a union leader, as they say, the honeymoon was over with my wife. Many times she didn't understand the job of a leader, of her husband, because I'd simply give her the pay envelope for a week's work without overtime or sometimes even without Sunday pay or with days lost. That definitely wasn't enough to cover the expenses of the household. I think that has been the chief reason for so many of the separations of compañeros and their wives at that time. Especially in these crisis years, I've seen many compañeros who have lost their spouses, fundamentally I think because of economic problems. I was lucky to keep mine, but there were many problems and troubles. My wife even came to believe that I had another woman. Like any woman, when her husband doesn't come home to sleep two or three times a week, it's normal that she might think that. But back then, there wasn't any time for thinking about another compañera because you were committed to the responsibilities you had assumed.

At that time, I wasn't lucky enough to have breakfast with my wife and children, nor lunch or supper either. I'd get up early and the kids would be sleeping and my compañera would serve me my cup of tea and my two slices of bread. I'd leave and I don't know if she'd have breakfast with my kids. At lunchtime, just the same, I'd eat lunch in the factory or many times on the street, and often there wasn't even any lunch for me. The same thing would happen with supper. In other words, I'd arrive at two or three in the morning when my woman was already asleep and I had to serve myself whatever there was left in the house. For the longest time, I didn't have a chance to break bread with my children.

16

Retirement

Political Disillusion, New Horizons

I thought about retiring from the company when I saw that people were getting tired of us. I saw that in the years 1978–79, when the clasista sector of the union became divided. The breakup of the clasistas was the result of a breakup of a group on the left, specifically of Vanguardia and Clase Obrera, and later of Trinchera Roja and Vanguardia. When this happened, the groups in the rank and file began to fight over the secretary general's office of the union. I think it was a bad way to go. We always handled the political disagreements that we might have had with dignity, without trying to see each other as enemies, but other people didn't show the same respect.

We were about to support a candidate for secretary general from another group, but they proposed a name which we didn't agree with and finally we didn't come to an agreement. Then we held the elections and they beat us, but the following year the opposition to the clasistas beat that group.

Again, I thought about quitting when my comrades from Metal Empresa were fired (like those from other sectors in large numbers) because of the 19 July 1977 strike. On that occasion, I was the subsecretary general of the union. With so much hostility from the military government headed by Morales Bermúdez, neither the national organization nor the federations could implement an active strategy to defend the fired leaders, who were the best group leading the workers' movement and the popular movement. That's what happened. I saw it close up because I had been in the Unified Command of the la lucha together with Andrés Luna Vargas of the Confederación Campesina del Perú, with César Barreda from Sindicato Unico de Trabajadores de la Educación del Perú, with Néstor Pastor from the CGTP, and so many other leaders. In the meetings, a response wasn't agreed upon.

After the internal breakups of the parties, finally there was the breakup of ARI (Alianza Revolucionaria de la Izquierda). All of this, seeing the pathetic Diez Canseco crying the afternoon when the ARI broke up. The UDP (Unidad Democrática Popular) was destroyed and then I got involved as a way of trying to save the UDP and trying to get it on the ballot. With only a few hours to go, they managed to get their list of candidates on the ballot. I was fortunate to get three male compañeros and a female compañera to complete the list. It was at that point I chose to quit my job even without any prospects. I realized that I wasn't going to be worse off than I already was.

I quit with reduced compensation because, as a labor leader, I hadn't been able to get overtime, and many times I missed out on the Sunday pay. Since the wages that you earned were insufficient to cover sickness or school supplies for the children, I had asked for loans and advances which were discounted from my severance pay. When I left I set up the Olympic Shop, which I still own on Avenida Argentina.

I now see that when I was working at Metal Empresa and when I was a union leader, I didn't know anything about the cost of manual labor. I didn't know how much the labor of a worker cost the company or how much the company charged per kilo of finished structures, boilers, and ships. I never found that out. Once I left, I realized that we had completely overlooked some things. Every day I saw cases of compañeros who were leaders who had been fired and were working on their own, for example, by producing glass products (glasses and jars). They said that they didn't know anything about production costs either. I think this wasn't so much neglect on our part as the way they had trained us. I especially think that for the great majority of us on the Left, this was an oversight by the leaders.

In that sense, I think that the country is entering a new phase in which serranos and provincial people have begun to take the first steps toward not only leading a union but also being able to run a shop or a company. Right now, most of us are crawling. But those who will come after us will come with a different outlook and, in that sense, with new prospects for the future in Peru. All these people, in new places, and by the hundreds, are working on their own. A time is going to come, and I hope it is soon, when there are new prospects for national industry and for decentralized development.

17

The Unión Grauina
The President Is Also a Peruvian

There was a person from my province who worked near my shop, but we didn't know each other. He only knew my brothers. He invited them to a meeting for former residents of the Curpahuasi district, and they told him that they had a brother with experience as a union leader. Then this person from my home province gave them an invitation for me.

With the invitation my brothers gave me, I attended a meeting. More than seventy people went. A worker affiliated with the political party APRA presided over the Organizing Committee. Lawyers and teachers shared the other positions. At the meeting, someone said that we shouldn't play politics. Then, I asked to speak. I stood up on a chair because I was in the back, and I explained how our actions are influenced by politics and that this was not a bad thing. It caused a stir and people turned around to look at me.

During an intermission, the Organizing Committee called me over to talk with them. They offered me "whatever position I might want," but they already had set up the list. I didn't accept. I told them that the masses elect their leaders and that's how it was. By majority vote, the assembly elected me the first president of the District Social Center of Curpahuasi and Anexos [outlying areas], an organization that had just been formed by that assembly.

Our first task was to look for the resolution that created the Curpahuasi district. Nobody had a copy of it, not even the members of the Organizing Committee. Therefore, I had to go and look for it in the National Library until I found it. During the two years that I carried out my duties, we did three or four district news programs. I rented a half hour of time from a radio program every day for seven months. We cut a record of *huayano* [traditional folk music of the sierra], with some anti-imperialist content in the lyrics. But above all, we drew up a list of demands for the district by sector: education, health, transportation, etc., that later served as the basis for the list of demands from Grau province. In the Board of Directors' meetings we looked at the problems of each town, area by area. It was a very important job because in doing this we realized that, as residents in the capital, we weren't contributing anything to the region where we had been born.

In November 1980, we elected delegates to the Unión Grauina (Union of Grau Province), who were like union delegates to the Federación. The basic activities of the Unión Grauina were cookouts and parties. We proposed that we should be actively helping our people. People from the province asked the Unión to complain to the authorities. Then we began to send letters to teachers and the authorities asking them to improve the treatment of peasants, that abuses be stopped, and it produced results because the abuses decreased. At that time, like always, I maintained my relation with the party [Vanguardia Revolucionaria], and one of its lawyers helped me to prepare the documents for the authorities. Also, I talked a lot with Andrés Luna Vargas, who encouraged me. He thought that the work we were doing was good. Later, they elected me to a position on the Provincial Social Center of the Unión Grauina.

The delegates who were elected to the Unión had to work to strengthen it. We thought that, through the institution, the eleven districts could be shown how to direct their demands to the government authorities. After intensive work on drafting a list of demands, the document was taken by the delegates to the assembly of the Unión Grauina. As president, I made a presentation about the problems of the Curpahuasi district which impressed the delegates from the province of Grau. Our documents served as a guide to the rest of the districts. They began to make their own suggestions and develop their own documents. Finally, the Unión Grauina compiled everything and produced a final document to be presented to the government. This document was submitted to the Senate Chamber, to the Chamber of Deputies, and to the president of the republic on the anniversary of the Unión Grauina. That coincided with the anniversary of the Curpahuasi district and that was that.

In the course of these steps and adventures, we identified the need for a branch of Cooperación Popular [a social welfare and employment program] to be created in Grau Province. The Acción Popular government was implementing the program and with the help of Congressman Gilberto Sea, the branch was created. A local organization of Cooperación Popular was established in Grau, but with persons who weren't from the province. We objected to that and suggested that those charged with holding the three decisive positions be *grauinos*. On our part, we proposed the names of those who we thought should hold those posts and we managed to get the officials changed. We decided at a meeting who ought to travel and made this decision without consulting the people who had been chosen to go. If they refused, we were ready to make the sacrifice of traveling and taking charge of these duties, to take over as officials of Cooperación Popular ourselves. For us, it was imperative that the grauinos be the ones who held those posts. But we were fortunate in that the people from our province who we had chosen accepted and quit their jobs. These negotiations lasted nearly twenty-five days, and the sacrifice that they made was very important. I think it was the first time that an organization of provincial residents in the capital took such action. At the time, we were overjoyed at having obtained what we wanted. I have vivid memories of leaving the congress, near the CONACO building. We had held a meeting with about thirty persons who had attended to congratulate and greet us. We surprised them with the election of compañeros from our province who were even quitting their jobs and leaving their wives and children to make a contribution to the people of Grau.

As this was coming to an end, a general assembly was called. Many grauinos attended, including the three named by us to go to our province. It was decided at that meeting to give them moral and organizational support through the Unión Grauina. For that purpose, the Curpahuasi district proposed organizing a mayors' convention at the provincial level of Grau, back at home. The idea was to introduce these officials of Cooperación Popular to the mayors, who would then give them all the necessary support. This proposal from Curpahuasi was accepted at the meeting of the Unión Grauina and it included a deadline for organizing and holding the convention. All the residents of each institution plus a delegate from each district had to attend. There was close coordination with Mayor Valverde. Documents were prepared with the expectation that they would be signed by the mayors and be presented to the appropriate authorities in the offices of Corporación de Desarrollo de Apurímac as well as here in the capital. Finally, the trip was taken and it was a very wonderful experience. We arrived in Grau in just one day. Many people, especially the opposition, said that the government had subsidized our tickets, but that's not how it was. We took our plane to Cuzco, from Cuzco a taxi to Abancay, and from there, yes, there were two pickup trucks to take us to Grau.

On that day we happened to meet Valverde, who was lost in Abancay. He hadn't gotten in contact with a single mayor. Then, through Cooperación Popular and Corporación del Desarrollo de Apurímac, we succeeded in having the authorities contact the mayors, and in some cases, we took the check ourselves to each district for the purpose of getting the attention of the mayors and making contact with them.

When we arrived in Grau, there were peasants there who had come from different communities to ask for tools. The new officials who had just been appointed didn't even have an office nor was there a desk or chair but there was a large amount of tools, corrugated iron, and even provisions. They wouldn't take the initiative to hand out these materials so then for two days we ourselves gave away the tools to all the peasants, leaving the warehouse, which was once full, completely empty. Some of the peasants thought we were God. Really, our people are a forgotten lot. We had peasants who were crying because they were given six spades, six picks, six carts, or six wheelbarrows. There were peasants who for the first time in their lives found out what corrugated iron was. That work was extraordinary. What can we say? Those officials were like brothers to us, our compañeros, because they gave us their full support even though we were like their bosses, although we never thought of ourselves as such. For their part, they deserved all our gratitude.

The mayors' meeting took place in Grau and we had the complete support of the authorities, of the church, of the teachers, and even of police force from Grau. We had their protection at all times. Mayor Valverde didn't even send a note to excuse his absence despite the fact that it was a mayors' meeting. This gentleman didn't attend and stayed in Abancay. Américo Oblitas, Valverde's assistant, took charge. The problems of each district were analyzed at the meeting and the real situation of the provincial capital itself was evaluated. We had electricity only until 10:30 at night. After that time, we lit twenty candles in the mayors' assembly. The discussion and the debates were very important, and finally a document was drafted about the needs of each district, by area and sector. Finally, the meeting agreed that Jesús Zúñiga was the best qualified person to draft the final documents and that he, through the Unión Grauina, would be the person to present the documents to Corporación del Desarrollo de Apurímac. I did this in my hometown, where, working in peace and quiet, I finally drafted the last document to be presented to Corporación del Desarrollo de Apurímac. The document was received by the Corporación's president, Hernán Portilla. Hernán was truly a person who supported me a lot. He told me: "Here you can have my office with three or four secretaries at your disposal. Jesús, this is a job which deserves complete support. I wish that the rest of the provinces would be concerned about this kind of work. It's the best gift for your province." These were Hernán's words verbatim, but I didn't make further use of his office and I left the documents there.

After the trip, an evaluation meeting was held here in the capital in which I presented the recorded comments of the mayors from the districts and an interview I did with Hernán Portilla. The assembly became silent. It was a revelation to them. I think that many grauinos had just come to the realization recently that they were from Grau; they had just realized that they were serranos, provincials. I saw more than one head lift up with pride. This evaluation meeting was very important. My proposal to Telósofo Berríos, the president of the Unión, was that he should take the document to the president of the republic so that the government might know that we also have needs to be addressed. We had already had the experience of presenting documents to the congressional caucuses of Izquierda Unida and APRA, but it had never produced any results and we got no feedback. In other words, the documents had been just filed away. With that experience in mind, the president of the Unión and I chose to present the documents through the appropriate channels. This proposal by the leadership was accepted and the documents were prepared. A commission was formed just in time for the anniversary of the province of Grau. In coordination with congressmen, we landed a meeting with the president of the republic.

In those documents we not only focused on the problems in the province of Grau but also on the department of Apurímac. It was a wide-ranging document, sector by sector, but done without prior consultation with the delegates because there wasn't enough time. I prepared a thirteen-point document. One of the points, the central one, was that a majority of the *apurimeños* wanted a National University of Apurímac to be founded. It made no sense that in Apurímac there's a private university when everyone knows full well that the peasantry lacks the economic means and isn't in any position to pay for its children to attend school there. It made no sense to have only a private university. In that document also, one of the points was the creation of branches of Cooperación Popular in the provinces of Aymaraes, Antabamba, Cotabambas, and

Chincheros. Chincheros is a recently created province in which Acción Popular set up its headquarters, but nevertheless Acción Popular never gave real support to the people. It just invoked the name of the people. In that meeting, these thirteen points that expressed the demands of apurimeños were for the most part accepted by the government. A whole series of benefits was won as a result of this document: tractors, compressors, and surveying instruments (which are scarce in the region). In this sense, we acknowledge that whatever the province of Grau has gotten so far is thanks to the efforts of the authorities, the peasants, and the many provincial people residing in the capital who gave all their support to get these things which are so necessary for our province.

Some identified me as an Acción Popular party member or an agent of the government who spoke the same language as Belaúnde. They must have had their reasons for seeing it this way, and one has to respect these opinions. I'd say that the experience of not missing out on an organization like Cooperación Popular was crucial. We made it work under the direction of our local people and at the same time we decided who should lead it. I think it was a mistake of leaders and advisers from other provinces that they failed to take stock of the situation in the same way.

But getting back to our meeting with the president, right that same day I prepared a handwritten draft with the thirteen main points. At the Confederación Campesina del Perú, they helped me to make a final copy just a little while before the meeting. Then I introduced myself at the meeting with the president of the Unión and I showed him the main outline. I spoke to him and he approved the document and signed it. For the meeting itself, it was surprising how they treated us at the palace. They frisked us carefully, and finally only the persons with jackets and ties were let in. There were only four of us who had a jacket and tie, but there were five of us altogether. And we thought that we were all going to get in. I was in the first row with the documents in my hand because the president of the Unión had ordered that I be the one to make the arguments and I had the folder in my hand. In view of this impasse, our congressman said, okay, you have to make an exception for Jesús because he's the leader. My answer to the aide-de-camp was to tell him, well okay, many of us are coming from our places of work and we haven't had time to go home and put on a jacket and tie, and in many cases, we don't even have one, right? Then, after consultations, he came out and said, okay, six persons are going to get in, but we had made it a point that everybody get in.

I was in the first row and my response to the congressman was also very clear: that they should not let everyone in just for the sake of Jesús Zúñiga, but rather that they respect a delegation coming from Grau Province that represented many towns. Finally, the aide-de-camp came out again, and he appealed to us. And I said to him, "Well, why does our president have to be ashamed of his fellow Peruvians if the president is one of us and he's Peruvian?" I think those words got to him. They made him feel guilty, and after a few seconds he returned and said that to avoid problems, he'd let everybody go in and he showed us in and that's how the meeting was. Taking this position was very important because I saw the satisfaction on the faces of my countrymen on getting into the palace and at least shaking the president's hand. Not many have had the good fortune or the privilege of arguing and putting forth our viewpoints about our towns, about the University of Apurímac, and we handed over these documents making the argument that in Grau there were defenseless children and orphans and other points of this kind. Three days later, I think, the president sent us a communique, in which he gave priority to the creation of Cooperación Popular in some provinces.

18
Defending the Absent

Being a union leader right now must be very difficult and sensitive by virtue of the situation we're living in. That's why a union leader must exhibit discipline, real discipline, and that comes through political organizations. Because if they don't, I think that the crisis of hunger and misery that we are living in and the absolute neglect on the part of the parties of Izquierda Unida will get the best of them and they'll lose. In this vein, I'd recommend that leaders place all their confidence in their own social class, that they trust the workers who put their trust in them. Leaders must know how to lead on the basis of loyalty. Directing the fortunes of a union is no joke; it's defending the daily bread of children, of children and wives who don't have any voice in the union assemblies. In other words, leaders are the defenders of people who may be absent from the assemblies but who indirectly place their trust in them. My recommendation is that union leaders be loyal to their compañeros and, above all, to the families of those compañeros who place all their trust in them.

PART III

Conclusion

19

Unstable Processes, Radical
Actions, Precarious Relationships,
and Relative Identities

The lives of these men—like those of all of the people of Peru—unfolded
as they struggled to make a place for themselves in the midst of distressing
insecurity and social instability. In the face of deteriorating conditions in
the countryside, these men set out on an adventure. They left behind their
traditional life in the countryside and entered a completely foreign urban
world. They imagined the city as a place for advancement. The move put
an end to centuries of tradition. It transformed those who were Andean
shepherds in their childhood into street peddlers, workers, or small in-
dustrialists. As Jesús' life shows, successive moments in one and the same
biography embody the historic changes that have taken place in Peru.

These men moved to a city where most of Peru's economic surplus was
concentrated. Lima retained the profits generated by mining and fishing
exports and was the principal center of growth for manufacturing. The
socioeconomic reality of Lima, however, also turned out to be marked by
unstable processes and chaotic situations. The city depended on the surplus from the primary export sector. That sector eventually lost its economic dynamism, as did the agricultural sector, which deteriorated and
led to the flight of the rural population to the city. Industrial growth accel-
erated and then entered a crisis. The crisis was aggravated by the failure of
the neoliberal policies of Belaúnde, inflation, and the deterioration in the
quality of urban life. All this was part of the landscape of urban life in the
1980s. For the urban population employed in industry, overall conditions
worsened and participation in unstable commercial and service occupations in the informal sector of the economy grew.

Becoming a worker when industrial employment was on an upswing
during the 1960s and 1970s meant achieving two major goals in an insecure and changing society like Peru: access to a minimally acceptable

income and, after 1970, job security. Added to this was the chance of learning a trade that could open up more prospects for the future. For the migrants who made up the overwhelming majority of industrial workers, achieving the status of a worker was seen as a definite improvement. Because of all this, industrial employment was not just valued in itself. For many migrants, industrial work represented one stop in a journey to realize the ideal of economic independence. It was an ideal forged early in their family and provincial experience.

The case study of Metal Empresa shows how factory workers came face-to-face with the commercial logic of the firm. While the company's external relations were organized according to market principles, its treatment of labor was despotic. It involved strict controls over production and speedups on the factory floor. These relations included the argolla system. It was a mechanism for inducing cooperation from a select group of workers while exercising despotic control over the rest of the workforce. The group was established on the basis of cronyism; the personnel manager recruited people preferentially from his home province and granted them special privileges in exchange for their cooperation.

Keeping the job and learning a skill were individual aspirations not easily realized by workers. This was especially true for the migrants, who were disadvantaged by their poor education. Competing with other workers to aquire legal status as a permanent worker and for consideration from the bosses for overtime hours and other benefits created an atmosphere of rivalry between serrano and criollo workers. The mutual resentment stemmed from differing approaches to getting ahead on the job — the serrano proclivity for physical labor and obedience to authority versus the criollo advantage in education and knack for developing informal ties to the bosses. Workers reproached each other, either for their absolute obedience to the bosses (as in the criticisms by criollos of serranos) or because of their unwillingness to work (as in the criticisms by serranos of criollos). These rivalries, however, did not become overwhelmingly important in factory life because workers shared the same reality; they were subordinates in a despotic system. They were marginalized and unable to demand improvements that ran contrary to the company's interests.

As the number of workers in the factory grew, the argolla system ran up against its own limits as a control mechanism. A group of politically active workers was able to lay the foundations of a skeletal organization that, in turn, served as a basis for the subsequent formation of a union.

This was possible because the workers came to recognize that they shared the same situation: they were not only producers of useful products, but they were also producers of wealth. On that basis, they were able to assert their rights to higher wages.

The workers consolidated their union when the practice of employer lockouts was outlawed. The lockout had been part of a system to control workers that included despotic treatment and the argolla system. The whole system revolved around a threat: a threat of exclusion. The threat of exclusion had been used effectively and widely to subordinate and control individuals. It was practiced by all institutions in Peruvian society. It was a powerful threat because of the limited opportunities that existed for lower-class people in Peru. Once the workers acquired job security in 1970, however, this threat lost its effectiveness. The complete dependence of workers on the company gave way to a mutual dependence in which the company had to live up to its obligations to the workers it hired. The union consolidated its power in this new context. Once the threats to individual workers were minimized by job security, the union could use the strike as a means of pressuring the firm.

With their union in place, the workers were transformed. They went from being wage earners, who could be treated like nonentities, to workers. Workers were producers of wealth and persons with rights vis-à-vis the company. After years of despotic treatment by the company, clasista unionism unequivocally affirmed the dignity of workers and established their rights.

The union asserted the right of everyone to receive benefits by virtue of being workers and not because of their ties of personal dependence on the company. The union affirmed common and equal benefits for all. Once this principle was established, the real contradictory nature of wage relations, long obscured by dependence and subordination, became clear to workers. Workers affirmed their status as workers in a variety of ways. They won substantial wage increases. They sought and won decent working conditions and more dignified treatment from company authorities. They organized protests. In dealing with mostly migrant workers who lacked any working-class traditions, the union used its organization and its struggles to affirm that workers stood on common ground. The union sought to downplay the *differences* among workers—whether those be ethnic, regional, or by trade and position in the factory. This homogenization was reinforced by the development of a union life that involved acts of solidarity, exercises in organization, and the inauguration of traditions and commemorative dates with high symbolic value (like the anniversary of the union and May Day).

An essential component of the identity of clasista unionism was its radicalism. Rather than just acting as an organization that negotiated with the company on behalf of workers, the union was an organization for la lucha —the workers' struggle to impose their will on the company. Certainly struggle would not have been necessary if the company had been willing to recognize the workers' union as a legitimate actor, akin to a plaintiff seeking to negotiate the settlement of a lawsuit. But instead of negotiating and taking at least some of the workers' demands seriously, the company opted to try to prevent the formation of a union. It rejected negotiations with the workers and disregarded their demands. In this situation, the workers accepted the proposals of their clasista leaders—whose effectiveness was proven in practice. Clasista leaders urged workers to rely on a method capable of guaranteeing respect for their rights and an expansion of benefits: the strike, a method to exercise pressure collectively. Because the strike strategy was successful in establishing job security for workers, it was viewed widely as an effective tool.

La lucha also proved to be an effective strategy in the diverse environments in which the worker lived. It was applicable to one's role as a worker and as an urban settler. The heterogenous social milieu of city life was one of the principal factors that contributed to the relative character of working-class identity. The household economy might rest on diverse activities such as the worker's job, a small independent family business, and others. But opportunities for economic advancement were not only determined by an individual's performance. In the diverse ways in which a worker was integrated into city life both as a worker *and* an urban settler, he sought to broaden his economic horizons. He did so by associating himself with movements that mobilized and pressured business and the state to distribute greater economic benefits.

Waging la lucha in diverse environments gave birth to a variety of organizations in which the urban settler participated. These organizations relied on the capacity of their members to mobilize collectively. Disparities in the levels and effectiveness of collective action led to disparities in the distribution of resources. An urban settler might have a steady job in a factory, own land, have a house with electricity, and run a small independent family business, but at the same time, he might not have a property deed for his real estate or running water in his house.

The social interactions of urban settlers went well beyond those contemplated by clasistas. Sociability and collective action took place in heterogenous environments, assumed a variety of organizational forms, and produced disparities in the extension of rights. Urban dwellers were incorporated into socioeconomic and political structures in a multilayered, multisectoral way. This multisectoral incorporation of the urban dweller into city life is perhaps captured in the term *sectores populares*. The radicalism of the popular sectors was successful in expanding opportunities, heightening political participation, and extracting more benefits from the state.

In the workers' environment and among all the other popular sectors, the organized Left was at the forefront of la lucha. At the beginning of the 1970s, the Left was still not an important political force. With its origins in the diverse, radicalized sectors of the middle class, the Left came into its own by supporting the vast popular sectors that did not fall under the influence or control of existing parties. The Left provided the support and direction that allowed popular sectors to organize to struggle for their demands. Radical university students, the core constituency on the Left, took advantage of the vast opportunities available to organize among industrial workers. They took advantage of the opportunity to recruit those workers who had the best qualifications for becoming leaders. The party helped these select groups of workers to organize and lead their unions. In exchange, leftist parties incorporated union leaders into their ranks.

For clasista workers, union struggles were not just a means of winning benefits for the workers. In line with the positions staked out by parties, the struggles took on a political meaning as part of a strategy of opposition to the military government by the Left. Nonetheless, in an economic context where industry was booming, the struggles proved to be highly effective as a means of obtaining benefits. Through clasista leaders, a clientelistic bond between workers and the Left was established. Clasista union leaders would draw on the resources of the party to support the workers' organization. In exchange, workers supported their leaders and showed their support in their willingness to engage in radical mobilization. On the basis of workers' mobilizations, leftist groups competed among themselves to lead the political opposition to the military government.

Clasista unionism did indeed affirm the workers' identity. It broke up the argolla in the factory. It gave workers equal opportunities for participation. But inside the union organization, paternalistic relations based on the dependence of the workers on their leaders for direction and protection were replicated. Previously, workers were subjected to the despotic authority of the company. In the midst of new and insecure circumstances, workers established new relations of dependence with their union leaders. With union leaders acting as intermediaries, workers also entered into a relationship of dependence with leftist groups, which, in turn, encouraged workers to seek improvements in wages and working conditions by using the strategy of la lucha. This link resembled the traditional relationship between a caudillo and his followers. Workers delegated the responsibilities for decision making and management of the union to their leaders. In exchange, they supported leaders and took part in la lucha when leaders asked them to do so. This included the participation of workers in mass demonstrations. Workers participated not so much out of a sense of abstract political conviction but because of a sense of reciprocity; it was a way to repay the protection and benefits that clasista leaders had won. On the basis of these relations of dependence, clasistas practiced an authoritarian leadership style. They ignored those who disagreed with them and silenced dissenting voices. The threat of exclusion—a mechanism used by the company to subject the workers to industrial discipline—was used by the union leaders to impose their political agenda on workers.

On the basis of their control over workers, clasista leaders were able to link unions across companies and coordinate collective protests. La lucha was the common cause that brought the metallurgical unions together in the 1970s. For workers, the Federación Metalúrgica was not so much an expression of institutionalized trade unionism as it was an organization for taking collective action. Through their unions, the workers established relations of reciprocity. They supported each other in their company struggles, and they allied with each other to defend themselves against the state.

For diverse reasons, the strategy of la lucha eventually ran up against limits and became less effective as a means to expand workers' benefits. The exhaustion of la lucha precipitated a crisis between clasista leaders and workers and among metallurgical unions. The crisis demonstrated how precarious the links had been among the actors joined in la lucha. La lucha was based on personalistic ties and maintaining relations of reciprocity. When, as in the case of Metal Empresa, union leaders called upon workers for a radical mobilization that was not directly connected to expanding workers' benefits, workers stopped following leaders. In turn, when union leaders failed in their efforts at mass mobilization, they gave up their leadership positions. As the radical mobilization of the workers lost its importance as a political resource, leftist parties distanced themselves from the unions.

Clasismo also faced another limitation as a form of unionism. The conflict of interests that was at the heart of clasismo ideology—the conflict between employers and workers—animated and inspired the union in its fight against the exclusionary practices of firms. At the same time, this ideology dictated a certain view of the nature of the firm; that understanding was based on the idea of exclusion. From the viewpoint of clasismo, the firm was an entity that functioned exclusively in the interests of the owners, and its well-being was the responsibility of those owners. By conceptualizing the company as something that functioned in the sole interests of owners, however, workers limited their thinking about their relationship to the firm in the long run. With the onset of the economic crisis, the clasista notion of a firm undermined the credibility of employers. The company's explanations of the economic problems that business confronted were not accepted by workers. Workers failed to understand the complexities of the problems that businesses faced and staged more and more radical protests in the factories.

Clasismo was a proactive response to a situation of exclusion and contributed to the consolidation of workers' rights in Peru. It was a demand-centric conception of trade unionism in which problems were solved by requesting, then demanding, a response from the firm. Union activity focused on la lucha. The principles contained in clasismo limited workers' consciousness and imagination in adjusting to new and more complex circumstances such as those posed by the economic crisis and democracy in the 1980s. Rather than being an ideology used to devise strategies to organize workers and link them to other social groups, clasismo became an ideology that promoted trade unionism of the most combative sort. Politics, in turn, was defined as the art of organizing and devising strategies to win by extracting benefits through the threat of or the actual exercise of force. It was a vision in which negotiation and compromise were regarded as signs of weakness. The view fueled the many unfortunate and failed attempts of unions to resolve problems by escalating the level of conflict. At the same time, clasista ideas were applied to the state, which was defined as an entity identified with the interests of "enemies." As such, the state became the target of the same type of radicalized demand-making that workers directed toward employers. This belligerent radicalism became a source of immobilism in the workers' movement. Clinging to its glorious radical past, the workers' movement was unable to develop a realistic strategy in the context of the economic crisis of the 1980s. Ultimately, the dynamic of distrust and antagonism was replicated in the relations among workers—in the conflicts that involved the demands of skilled workers, the treatment of dissenters, and the partisan divisions among clasistas.

As unions lost their capacity to win concrete material gains for workers, workers turned away from unionism and began to look for individual ways to improve their lot. This surge in the desire of workers to abandon their status as wage earners and devote themselves to their own independent moneymaking activities was characteristic of Peru in the 1980s. Once salary gains and improvements in working conditions leveled off and companies began to downsize by offering severance packages, many workers seized the opportunity to start up their own businesses. Among migrants, this desire was something that made their status as workers seem relative; the desire was deeply rooted in the ideals of economic independence that they brought from the countryside. Unlike the limeño who became a worker, the migrant who became a factory worker did so as part of a process of overcoming obstacles and making progress. His final goal was to accumulate capital. As such, many migrants saw the factory as a stop on their journey where they could learn and save money. They postponed immediate gratification of their needs in order to advance their long-term objectives.

The 1980s were a period of historic change marked by economic crisis and political liberalism. Job insecurity and declining wages pauperized workers, forcing them to seek out incomes to supplement their wages. They did this by extending the workday by taking part-time jobs outside the factory, financing income-producing activities with factory wages, using the home to generate income, extracting income from other family members, and modifying household consumption in light of the new economic circumstances. Added to this problem were the frustrations in the factory that came with the economic recession and the loss of the union's importance as a representative and guarantor of the rights won by workers. To a great extent, that loss was a product of a widespread noncompliance with the provisions of collective contracts on the part of firms. The deterioration in economic and social conditions during the 1980s eroded working-class identification with trade unionism.

20
What Can You Hope For?
Jesús in the 1990s

In July 1999, Jesús met with Jorge Parodi once again. Jesús discussed his experiences in the years since the original publication of the book.

Times have been tough. Since the time of Alan García, you started to see industries closing and going bankrupt. In the same way, institutions like cooperatives, banks, and savings and loan companies where people kept all their money also went broke. In the end, people were left without their savings. I had some money from the Unión Grauina, not much, deposited in Mutual Perú. And as secretary general of my neighborhood association, I also had money in the Banco Hipotecario. We never got our money back from the bank. All those institutions ended up with the money that people deposited. Corruption was the rule in the time of Alan García. Corruption was institutionalized across the board, it was everywhere, and it included him. That's why he fled the country.

The hardships of the years can be seen clearly in the case of myself and my family. I once had eighteen to twenty people working in my shop. I ended up working with just my sons. All my compañeros that worked with me have gone on to do temporary jobs here and there, and that's what they survive on.

In the case of my sons, Carlos is the one who does metallurgical work on a contract basis. He does a lot of the same kind of jobs he learned as a young boy thanks to the support and help of the guys who worked with me. I am so grateful to them because they always treated my son like a nephew. He builds metal roofs and boats and does work with stainless steel, copper, and bronze. It's temporary contract work, and sometimes he can't get any at all. He's thirty-two years old and lives with his wife, Nelly, who is four months pregnant.

My son Pepe continues studying at the Universidad Nacional de Ingenienía, where he is on the faculty of mechanical and electrical engineering. He is twenty-seven years old. I hope he can finish his studies, be a good professional, and put his knowledge to good use for his country.

My daughter, María Isabel, is twenty-six years old. She went to study journalism at the Instituto Bausate y Meza. She studied seven or eight months. Then she had a bad experience, something that happens when you are young, right? She left pregnant and now has an eight-year-old daughter, Laura. My daughter ended up working with me, as a secretary and receptionist. Sometimes she helps in our specialty, boilermaking and welding.

My wife, María Salome, like all wives, suffers through the difficult periods, taking care of the kids and our home. Thanks to her help and the help of all the women of my neighborhood, we were able to get legal titles to lots of land for every family in our neighborhood, Asentamiento Humano "Cuadra 57 de la Avenida Argentina" in Callao. It happened two years ago, after forty years of trying.

For more or less forty-five years, thirty-two families have lived in my neighborhood. In 1962, we were recognized as a *barrio marginal* (marginal neighborhood). From that time on until two years ago, we were trying to achieve something we always wanted—an equal distribution of the neighborhood land into lots for every family. We now have provisional legal titles to the lots issued by the Callao provincial council. The final stage is to get a permanent title for everyone and collect the land payment from everyone. But in order to divide up the land in the neighborhood equally, we had to agree to new boundaries for the lots and we had to tear down our own houses, most of which had been made of adobe with wood roofs. Our houses had to be remade with mats and cardboard cartons.

Even though more than forty years have gone by, we still find ourselves lobbying for the installation of water and sewers from the company Sedapal. Currently, we only have one water pipe for the entire neighborhood. As far as sewers go, only about ten homes have installed some sort of indoor plumbing and the rest of the families go to the bathroom in cans or containers. We live like animals. This harsh reality is found not only in my neighborhood but in the great majority of neighborhoods in Lima, Callao, and the rest of the country.

Of the thirty-two families in my neighborhood, only two people have steady jobs. The rest of the men find temporary jobs, like unloading trucks. They look for jobs and sometimes find them only two or three times a week. My neighbors who are single mothers find work doing laundry, taking care of old people or children—and that's the way they support their families. You realize how poorly fed children are, not just in my neighborhood but across the country. And don't even mention the "Fuji-shock." It was so terrible. There was nothing to eat. There was a long period of time that we had to live on food donations from the mayor's office in Callao and Caritas del Perú (a charitable organization run by the Catholic Church). Trigol was a wheat product donated by international agencies. We had Trigol for breakfast. We had Trigol for lunch. We had Trigol for dinner.

The people who worked in my shop with me are like my own family. Together, we did work for the Fábrica Nacional de Licores and the Parque Industrial San Pedrito No. 1 and No. 2. The companies were owned by Señor Jacinto Poblete Vidal. We did expert work in boilermaking and making water tanks and distilling equipment. We worked with stainless steel, copper, and bronze. According to the technicians from the Banco de la Nación who came to inspect the work, they would have never imagined the equipment that we constructed could have been made in Peru. They thought I was a technician or supervisor of the company. When they found out that I was just contracted for the job, they congratulated me. They told me that my equipment was the best to be found in all the liquor plants of Peru—and that was regardless of the fact that they had been made out of secondhand materials cast aside by the company. For me, it was a very important learning experience and also seeing the way in which the company benefited from increasing its production. I was also proud that during the sales campaigns of July and December the company increased the number of employees hired by 100 percent.

Today, the Fábrica Nacional de Licoreres Poblete is not fully operational all the time. It has only two permanent supervisors and contracts workers on a temporary basis. What a difference from what it was before! There were between two hundred and four hundred workers, men and women, depending on the time of the year. Production fell off with the Fuji-shock and then with the importation of foreign liquors. The result was that I personally ended up without a job, as did everyone else who worked with me.

It's a shame. After so much effort and dedication and dealing with the arbitrary policies of the government, we have to start over again as if it were thirty or thirty-five years ago. And the conditions are worse than before. Not only did liquor production fall off, but industrial production of all kinds. So we looked for a way out in the only thing that we know how to do, and that is working with metals. The automobile companies are broke, the shipyards are bankrupt, and the companies that produce washing machines, refrigerators, and stoves are also broke. So, during the Fujimori government, I have not been able to find work, except for occasional odd jobs.

Despite all those difficulties, I was able to take advantage of my experience and knowledge and participate in developing equipment for industry. I have been working through the Consejo Nacional de Ciencia y Tecnología (CONCYTEC—National Council of Science and Technology), and they have supported me in working on three projects: building stainless steel grinding mills, building stainless steel pump screws, and designing a prototype of an automatic pantograph cutting machine. CONCYTEC gave me two thousand of the six thousand soles I needed to buy materials.

As a result of my work, I repaired water pumps for ten mining companies. As far as the mills go, I was able to sell five of them. I have not yet sold the automatic pantograph. I gained valuable experience so that now I can work with bigger equipment and better serve the needs of clients.

Twenty-five years ago I served as president of the Centro Social Distrital Curpahuasi and Anexos. The organization brought together Lima residents from eighteen different towns, and I was a delegate to the Centro Social Provincial Unión Grauina made up of former residents of fourteen districts of Grau Province. Through that organization, we came to see the utility of getting together all the district and provincial organizations, with the goal of studying the problems of education, health, agriculture, irrigation, and communication in the region. Our study was presented to the corresponding authorities at the departmental and national levels.

I was always an advocate of popular participation, and I was elected as president of Unión Grauina and served in a difficult period. There were two candidates for the post, and I was elected for two years. Through Unión Grauina, we reorganized all the district organizations of Lima residents and we promoted the creation of provincial organizations. The Federación was successful in getting the Nazca-Abancay-Cuzco highway paved and getting the Kunyac bridge built that connects the department of Cuzco with Apurímac. The Unión formed part of the departmental Federación of Apurímac that includes all the organizations of the department.

I'd say that the people made a mistake in reelecting Fujimori as president, especially given what the Fuji-shock meant. It wiped out many enterprises, and workers were fired in droves without even receiving their severance benefits. That is what happened to workers, and don't even talk about agriculture—where the great majority of Peruvians are employed. All this happened for the purpose of complying with agreements with the International Monetary Fund and the World Bank. The foreign debt is paid punctually to them at the cost of the hunger and poverty of our people. Then, there's the sale of strategic industries such as Telefónica [telephone service] to the Spaniards and Edelnor [electricity] to the Chileans. Today, those companies do whatever they like. They have a monopoly and there are no companies to compete with them. That shows that promotion of free competition is just talk. It doesn't exist in those two sectors. To pull all this off, political parties (whether they were on the Right or the Left) were demonized. They were accused of being traditional parties. That was the reason for the 5 April coup of 1992, when the army went into the streets to intimidate people. All this was nothing but a plan to keep themselves in power to better serve their masters, and without giving a damn about the people.

I see an extremely difficult future for this country. With national industry destroyed, what can you hope for? In all sectors of the economy, with the large sugar-producing cooperatives of the north destroyed, what can you hope for? Without support for agriculture, with the free import of foreign goods plus all the contraband, I hardly see any prospects for the future of this country. The young people find themselves in the worst situation, with no job prospects.

So what should we do? Look at this harsh reality that persists with each passing government, year after year. Rather than overcoming the difficulties, we Peruvians find ourselves in worsening circumstances. That's because those who govern do not represent the genuine interests of the Peruvian people. The only alternative at the national level to promote the reconstruction of the country is to work with local mayors and officials in the departments and provinces to launch a national emergency program. We should incorporate leaders from industry, agriculture, education, and

JESÚS IN THE 1990S

health and get down to the basics that people are demanding. To this end, the departmental Federación de Apurímac is making contacts with departmental leaders from Junín, Ayacucho, Huancavelica, and Madre de Dios, with the hope of extending contact throughout the rest of the departments. We think that this is the route that we should follow in order to launch an alternative to save and rebuild the nation.

Epilogue

I finished writing this book in 1985 after completing the research in 1984. At that time, the tendencies that I described were just starting to manifest themselves. For some radical groups, my analysis was discomforting. They rejected it because I pointed to processes that questioned the existence of a solid working-class identity, a strong and growing trade unionism, and a covenant between unions and leftist parties. It was a different time — very distinct from current circumstances where the Left around the world is in retreat. In the mid-1980s, the future of Peru still seemed to be linked inextricably to the future of the Left.

In the ensuing years, Peru suffered through traumatic events. During the government of President Alan García (1985–90), economic crisis and terrorist violence became a devastating, all-encompassing reality that no one could have imagined earlier in the decade. Accomplishments that were so important in the 1970s, such as the growth of trade unionism, lost importance because of the corrosive effects of the economic crisis, political violence, and the failure of successive civilian governments to turn democracy into something more substantial than just electing public officials.

When I compare Peru's current situation to the tendencies that I described in 1985, the results are shocking. The conditions of working-class life have continued to deteriorate. Unions are weak. The relationships between unions and political parties are practically nonexistent. Working-class demands are rarely taken into account in government decision making.

Over the course of the last ten years, Peru's industrial sector has been in a prolonged crisis. The pursuit of economic development through import-substitution policies failed. The stagnation of the industrial sector is reflected in it own dramatic statistics. In 1992, the index measuring physical output in manufacturing fell twelve points below that of 1979 and nine points below that of 1985. Certain branches of industry registered declines even greater than the overall average. In the textile, clothing, and leather-making industries, output registered a fall in 1992 that

151

left it twenty-four points below its 1979 level. The metal and machine-making industry declined by forty points; the paper and publishing industry declined by sixty-six points.[1] As a consequence of this fall in industrial production, industrial employment declined. The index of manufacturing employment in 1992 fell thirty-one points below that of 1980.[2]

The stagnation in industry, along with other sectors of the economy, had diverse effects on workers. The structure of urban employment changed. This was evident in the growing informalization of the economy and employment. There was a deterioration in the standard of living of workers. Trade unions lost their capacity to lobby effectively for their members, and their members' attachment to a working-class identity eroded.

The stagnation of the modern and dynamic sectors of industry produced a notable increase in informal employment (i.e., employment in commercial, service, or manufacturing enterprises with a workforce of ten or fewer people). Between 1981 and 1992, formal employment in metropolitan Lima fell from accounting for 60.7 percent of the labor force to 38.5 percent. In the same time period, informal employment grew from 32.8 percent to 56.6 percent of the labor force.[3] There was a notable increase in street vending in Lima. From 1970 to 1990, street vendors went from accounting for 2.5 percent of the economically active population to 13.1 percent.[4] In short, the reduction of employment in manufacturing, the notable increase in microenterprises, and the expansion of street vending constituted key changes in the character of the labor market.

Moreover, as a result of the crisis and government mistakes in the management of economic policies, workers suffered an unprecedented deterioration in their standard of living. In 1992, the average real wages of a worker in the private sector were only 27.4 percent of what they had been in 1980 and 45 percent of what they had been in 1985. In 1993, the legal minimum wage was 15 percent of what it had been in 1980 and 28 percent of what it had been in 1985.[5] The deterioration is also evident in the statistics on underemployment. In metropolitan Lima, underemployment increased sharply from 26 percent in 1980 to 75.9 percent in 1992. Among the underemployed, acute underemployment increased from 7.1 percent in 1980 to 33.6 percent in 1992.[6]

Under these conditions, it is not surprising that labor unions could no longer effectively engage in their traditional activities, especially strikes. In the first half of the 1980s, workers faced a situation that was distinct from that in years past. Instead of seeking to ward off a loss of benefits and hold onto jobs, the immediate reaction of unions was to stage a strike. In the initial period of President Fernando Belaúnde's government (1980–85), strikes proliferated. In 1981–82, the number of strikes surpassed the previous record established in 1973. But the recession of 1983–84 made strikes less effective. In some cases, strikes were even beneficial for firms because the work stoppages allowed employers to save on wages for a few days. By this time, unions faced an abysmal situation. Some businesses closed altogether; others fired workers or fell behind in paying wages. Unions imagined that businesses would have to yield if they could mount pressures beyond a simple strike, and they sometimes took extreme measures. In 1984, no less than fourteen unions took over and occupied diverse locales that included factories, churches, and other public spaces. Three unions staged hunger strikes. One union took a cabinet minister as a hostage.[7]

Unions backed off from these tactics when it became evident that even the most radical measures were not enough to reverse the effects of a recessionary economic situation. That is why, after surviving yet another recession after the failure of the populist policies of President Alan García, many previously combative unions sought to come to understandings with business. They accepted proposals that had been unacceptable in the past, from agreeing to temporary shutdowns of plants to reductions in work schedules.[8] Strike activity fell. The number of workers involved in strikes in manufacturing was 112,000 in 1980. That figure dropped to 43,000 in 1985 and fell to 41,000 in 1990. In 1992, only 34,000 workers were affected by strikes.[9]

Even though the strongest unions managed to defend themselves under adverse circumstances, many of their demands failed to have an impact on government policy. Whether it was under the "liberal" model of Belaúnde or the "populist" model of García, governments imposed a policy of wage ceilings through the Ministry of Labor. Employers used these ceilings to control their costs. When workers protested the closing of factories, the layoffs, and business's failure to comply with labor laws, both business and government remained inflexible and dismissive in their attitudes.[10]

After implementing a shock policy to stabilize the economy and eradicate the hyperinflation left behind by the populism of Alan García, President Alberto Fujimori enacted new regulations that weakened the power of unions even more. In December 1991, Fujimori signed a bill passed by the legislature that made it easier for companies to fire personnel. In July 1992, Fujimori enacted a law affecting collective agreements. The law obligated unions to renegotiate all current collective agreements; it also established new legal requirements that severely limited the unions in the exercise of their rights. According to the International Labor Organization (ILO), the decree established excessive restrictions on the right to strike. In response to the outcry by the Peruvian unions, the ILO condemned the restrictive aspects of the law.[11] In 1993, a regulation by the Ministry of Labor clarified the scope of the Ley de Facultades del Empleador (Law of Employer Entitlement). The law allows an employer to void a collective contract.[12]

It is now difficult, if not impossible, for workers to be heard. It is difficult for them to participate in politics and express their views. They have been unsuccessful in pressuring governments to turn away from policies that hurt workers the most. Paradoxically, from the 1980s onward, Peru was supposed to be in the process of establishing democracy. Yet democracy produced a growing rift between workers and the political world. It is a breach that workers have sometimes attempted to close with desperate acts—as in the 1984 case of a glass factory union that occupied offices in the congress in order to pressure the Ministry of Labor to intervene in an employer's lockout of workers. Peruvian workers have lived and still live in a strange democracy—a democracy that rests on silencing its subjects.

One of the factors that contributed to the difficulties that unions faced in seeking political redress in their conflicts was the rift that developed between unions and their traditional party allies on the Left. With the return to democracy, leftist leaders found that their old discourse about the exclusionary character of the state no longer fit. The new democratic regime did open up new spaces for the inclusion of leftist parties in political life. There were new venues for participation—specifically the congress and municipal governments. These new spaces were far removed from the realm of trade unionism and required constant attention from leftist party leaders who were seeking to broaden their electoral base.[13]

The distance between unions and parties became even more acute, however, as parties were displaced by the new political leadership of Alberto Fujimori. In the midst of economic crisis and guerrilla violence, Fujimori appeared on the scene with an agenda that emphasized establishing political order, but doing so without the involvement of the traditional political parties. The political isolation of unions produced another desperate initiative by them. Given the Fujimori government's lack of response to protests by the ILO, Peruvian unions lodged a complaint with the United States government. The grievance was filed formally through the AFL-CIO in June 1993. The grievance was lodged in reference to a 1984 commercial law in the United States which mandated that certain types of preferential tariff treatment could be extended only to countries that abided by international agreements on labor rights. The Peruvian unions believed that Fujimori's labor laws effectively violated international agreements and that the United States should rescind tariff privileges from Peru.

Meanwhile, unions were being weakened by difficulties in maintaining their membership. This was the result of diverse measures taken by the Fujimori government to make labor contracts more "flexible." The liberalization of labor laws allowed employers to contract workers in ways that departed dramatically from the previous legal practices that had ensured that workers could acquire seniority and job stability. Alan García's government had already opened the door to the liberalization of labor laws by making it easier for companies to hire temporary workers. Fujimori went further by making it legal for businesses to take on temporary personnel through subcontracting agreements with employment agencies or other firms. These arrangements allowed companies to avoid any legal responsibility or liability vis-à-vis the temporary workers. Along with this, employers introduced new labor practices such as employing workers as part-timers while forcing them to take extra shifts or splitting up their labor force by dividing up an enterprise into separate companies.

All these developments weakened unions. In some cases, the new rules of the game impeded the formation of a single union in a firm because all the workers technically did not work for the same firm — some workers were tied to subcontracting firms while others were not. In other cases, although it was legally possible to form a single union, the presence of many temporary or part-time workers made it impossible. Temporary and part-time workers normally are pressured by employers not to join a union; and if they joined the union, they ran the risk that their contracts would not be renewed. Moreover, workers sometimes are offered incentives for not joining the union. Companies have been known to offer wage increases to workers who stay out of the union.[14] On the other hand, unions have not been very interested in including temporary workers in their ranks or engaging in coordinated action with them. In the last analysis, unions tend to see temporary workers as competitors, not allies.[15] Thus out of a total of 143,472 temporary workers in the 1990 labor force, only 17 percent were affiliated with a union.[16]

Predictably, one of the results of all these changes was a decline in the number of unionized workers in the labor force. In 1970, unionized workers accounted for 12.4 percent of the economically active population of Lima. In 1990, only 4.8 percent of Lima's workers were unionized.[17] Another important consequence was the reduction in the effectiveness of strikes as a bargaining tool for unions. Many companies simply contract temporary personnel during strikes through subcontracting firms authorized by the Ministry of Labor. Between January 1993 and June 1994, the ministry processed 663 requests by firms seeking to hire strikebreaking workers.[18]

It is not surprising that a feeling of intense frustration permeates working-class life. In a public opinion survey that I undertook with colleagues in the poor neighborhoods of Lima in 1990, 70 percent of these working-class respondents agreed with the statement that they had attained "little or nothing in life." Workers expressed a much higher level of dissatisfaction than office workers, shopkeepers, or students.

In this context of diminished rights, declining union organization, and frustration, what are the political attitudes of workers? How do they regard political parties and their leaders? What are their attitudes toward terrorism and political violence?

Peru's situation in the 1980s may have seemed ripe for attracting workers to guerrilla politics. The major guerrilla movement, Sendero Luminoso, made serious efforts to infiltrate unions and influence their orientations. Beginning in 1987, Sendero sought to develop its influence in poor urban neighborhoods and unions. This was in preparation for its expansion outside of its original base in the countryside. Sendero tried to launch a working-class organization, Movimiento de Trabajadores Clasistas. Terrorism was its method. Senderistas burned down some large factories. They assassinated businessmen and union leaders whom they considered to be traitors to the working class.

With a few exceptions, the actions by Sendero failed to arouse support from workers.[19] In 1991, as workers suffered the economic consequences of Fujimori's shock treatment policies, Sendero became more actively engaged in strikes and workers' protests. This included what Sendero referred to as the "selective execution" of businessmen and managers caught up in labor disputes.

Some observers argued at the time that the working class's approval of Sendero was growing and that this sympathy would turn into a more active attraction to the movement.[20] Such expressions of approval of terrorist violence were not something new in the working class. One found such expressions being voiced years earlier among working-class youth.[21] But the expressions of approval for terrorist violence that were rooted in the frustration and indignation did not translate into a willingness on the part of workers to join actively with Sendero. In reality, working-class membership in Sendero was low, just as it was among all lower-class groups in general.[22] Gonzalo Portocarrero's research on a factory in which Sendero tried to gain a foothold comes to the same conclusion about the relationship of workers and Sendero. Portacarrero concluded:

> There is bitterness and frustration among workers. It is also true that the weakness of the union acts as an impediment to channeling this discontent into mobilization or dialogue with company management. In the end, one has to take into account that workers identify with the egalitarianism of Sendero. Workers do not identify with businessmen—they can come to hate them. So much so that workers back off and wash their hands when Sendero attacks businessmen. However, all this does not mean that workers favor Sendero or make political violence into an option for themselves. In truth, they may view the crime itself with a certain sympathy and justified in terms of revenge. But it does not mean that they subscribe to the idea of violence as necessary or creative, as the principal weapon to create a new society.[23]

When they look to the future, workers do not feel hopeful if they imagine themselves remaining only as workers. When workers are asked about their prospects, they always refer to their hopes of becoming self-employed. Workers think of themselves less and less as workers and "tend to develop an image of themselves as future businessmen."[24] In the survey we did in 1990, 55 percent of workers said that they would prefer to be self-employed even if it meant that their income would be less by 10 percent. Only 15 percent of workers said that they hoped that their children would be workers. Thus, "now more than ever, to be a worker is relative."[25]

Appendix

Selected Political Chronology of Peru, 1968–1995

1968   Military coup d'état overthrows civilian government of President Fernando Belaúnde Terry. Beginning of "nationalist-revolutionary" government under the leadership of General Juan Velasco Alvarado. Velasco government is referred to as "Phase One," the most radical phase, of the Peruvian military experiment.

1969   Government enacts agrarian reform law.

1970   Enactment of Law of Security of Employment that created new labor regulations. Enactment of Industrial Community Law mandating employee profit sharing, stockholding, and participation in management of firms.

       Beginning of significant expansion in unionization of industrial labor force; most of the unions affiliated with Federación de Trabajadores de la Industria Metalúrgica del Perú founded in the period 1970–72.

1975   Poor economic performance; popular unrest and riots in Lima.

       General Velasco removed as president and replaced by General Francisco Morales Bermúdez. Bermúdez government is referred to as "Phase Two" of the military regime, more repressive and conservative than the previous Velasco government.

1976   Confederación General de Trabajadores del Perú withdraws its support of the government in protest of Morales Bermúdez's austerity policies.

1977   General strike called in July to protest government economic measures and repression. Seven hundred metallurgical union leaders fired from their jobs.

       Government announces its intention of returning to civilian rule by convoking elections for a constituent assembly to write a new constitution.

1978   One million workers participate in the general strike of May.

       Elections for constituent assembly held. Leftist parties win one-third of the seats.

1979   Constituent assembly writes a new constitution.

1980   Leftist parties unable to unite to form a single electoral front for the elections.

Presidential and congressional elections held. Fernando Belaúnde of Acción Popular is reelected to the presidency.

First appearance of guerrilla group Sendero Luminoso in department of Ayacucho.

1981   Belaúnde government makes piecemeal efforts to implement neoliberal economic measures.

1983   Onset of severe economic recession.

Alfonso Barrantes of the Izquierda Unida (IU) electoral front is elected mayor of Lima.

1985   Alan García of Alianza Popular Revolucionaria Americana (APRA) wins the presidential race in a single round when Alfonso Barrantes of IU declines to oppose him in the second-round run-off.

García government undertakes heterodox policies to reactivate the economy.

1986   Alfonso Barrantes loses Lima mayoralty to APRA candidate, Jorge del Castillo.

1987   President Alan García proposes the nationalization of domestic banks; the measure sparks widespread protests by business organizations and conservative parties and energizes the political Right.

1988   Economy begins to be affected by hyperinflation.

1989   The Izquierda Unida electoral front divides into two factions; each fields its own presidential and congressional candidates in the 1990 race.

1990   Political newcomer Alberto Fujimori defeats right-wing candidate Mario Vargas Llosa in the second round of the presidential election.

Fujimori administration undertakes program of economic stabilization and commits itself to neoliberal economic reform.

1991   Fujimori administration becomes increasingly critical of the congress and blames the legislature and judiciary for the lack of progress in economic reform and the war against terrorism.

1992   On 5 April, President Fujimori undertakes an auto-coup. The constitution is suspended, the congress is closed, and the judiciary is dismissed. A majority of the public approves the measures.

Under intense pressure from the international community, President Fujimori agrees to hold new elections for a congress that will function as a constituent assembly.

Sendero Luminoso's top leader, Abimael Guzmán, is captured in a police raid in Lima. The capture of Guzmán and other top leaders substantially weakens the guerrilla organization.

Fujimori's party, Cambio 90–Nueva Mayoría, wins a slim majority in the constituent assembly election.

1993   Constituent assemby controlled by the government majority writes a new constitution that allows for immediate presidential reelection.

New constitution is subject to a national referendum; it is approved by an extremely narrow margin.

1995   Alberto Fujimori reelected to the presidency and his party wins an absolute majority in congress.

Notes

Introduction to the English Translation

I would like to thank Paul Haslam and Michele Mastroeni for their excellent research assistance in the course of preparing this manuscript for publication. My own understanding of Peruvian working-class history has been greatly enriched by conversations with Luis Sirumbal of the Centro de Asesoría Laboral del Perú, CEDAL, in Lima. My thanks also go to David Perry, Ron Maner, and Trudie Calvert of the University of North Carolina Press for their work on this book.

1. Since the 1950s, the explosive growth of Lima has been the subject of extensive research and reflection. See José Matos Mar, *Desborde popular y crisis del estado: El nuevo rostro del Perú en la década de 1980* (Lima: Instituto de Estudios Peruanos, 1984). For analyses of social life and politics in the urban shantytowns, see David Collier, *Squatters and Oligarchs: Authoritarian Rule and Policy Change in Peru* (Baltimore: Johns Hopkins University Press, 1976); Henry Dietz, *Poverty and Problem-Solving under Military Rule: The Urban Poor of Lima* (Austin: University of Texas Press, 1980); Peter Lloyd, *The "Young Towns" of Lima: Aspects of Urbanization in Peru* (Cambridge: Cambridge University Press, 1980); Susan Lobo, *A House of My Own: Social Organization in the Squatter Settlements of Lima, Peru* (Tucson: University of Arizona Press, 1982); Carlos Iván Degregori, Cecilia Blondet, and Nicolás Lynch, *Conquistadores del nuevo mundo: De invasores a ciudadanos en San Martín de Porres* (Lima: Instituto de Estudios Peruanos, 1986); Susan Stokes, *Cultures in Conflict: Social Movements and the State in Peru* (Berkeley: University of California Press, 1995). For a recent treatment of social life in Lima, see the collected essays in Carmen Rosa Balbi, ed., *Lima: Aspiraciones, reconocimiento y la ciudadanía en los noventa* (Lima: Pontificia Universidad Católica del Perú, Fondo Editorial, 1997). For a volume that provides a wide-ranging look at the history and development of Peru, see Orin Starn, Carlos Iván Degregori, and Robin Kirk, eds., *The Peru Reader: History, Culture, Politics* (Durham, N.C.: Duke University Press, 1995).

2. There is an extensive literature on politics and policymaking during the Velasco military regime. The standard works on the period include David Booth and Bernardo Sorj, eds., *Military Reformism and Social Classes: The Peruvian Exprience* (London: Macmillan, 1983); David Chaplin, ed., *Peruvian Nationalism: A Corporatist Revolution* (New Brunswick, N.J.: Transaction Books, 1976); Carlos Franco, ed., *El Perú de Velasco* (Lima: Centro de Estudios para el Desarrollo y la Participación, 1989); Abraham F. Lowenthal, ed., *The Peruvian Experiment: Continuity and Change under Military Rule* (Princeton: Princeton University Press, 1975); Cynthia McClintock and Abraham F. Lowenthal, *The Peruvian Experiment Reconsidered* (Princeton: Princeton University Press, 1983); Henry Pease García, *El ocaso del poder oligárquico:*

Lucha política en la escena oficial, 1968–75 (Lima: DESCO, Centro de Estudios y Promoción del Desarrollo, 1986); George Philip, *The Rise and Fall of the Peruvian Military Radicals, 1968–76* (London: Athlone Press, 1978); and Alfred Stepan, *State and Society: Peru in Comparative Perspective* (Princeton: Princeton University Press, 1978).

3. For a discussion of the enactment and impact of the Law of Industrial Communities, see Evelyne Huber Stephens, *The Politics of Workers' Participation: The Peruvian Approach in Comparative Perspective* (New York: Academic Press, 1980); Giorgio Alberti, Jorge Santistevan, and Luis Pásara, *Estado y clase: La Comunidad Industrial en el Perú* (Lima: Instituto de Estudios Peruanos, 1977).

4. For a review of the development of trade unionism in this period, see Nigel Haworth, "Political Transition and the Peruvian Labor Movement, 1968–75," in *Labor Autonomy and the State in Latin America,* ed. Edward C. Epstein (Boston: Unwin Hyman, 1989), 195–218. For an overview of the historical evolution of the Peruvian labor movement and its impact on political life, see the discussion of the Peruvian case in Ruth Berins Collier and David Collier, *Shaping the Political Arena: Critical Junctures, the Labor Movement, and Regime Dynamics in Latin America* (Princeton: Princeton University Press, 1991).

5. For further discussion of the ideas and development of clasismo, see Denis Sulmont, *Historia del movimiento obrero peruano* (Lima: Editorial Tarea, 1977); Carmen Rosa Balbi, *Identidad clasista en el sindicalismo: Su impacto en las fábricas* (Lima: DESCO, Centro de Estudios y Promoción del Desarrollo, 1989); Carmen Vildoso, *Sindicalismo clasista: Certezas e incertidumbres* (Lima: EDAPROSPO, 1992); Gonzalo Portocarrero Maisch and Rafael Tapia Rojas, *Trabajadores, sindicalismo y política en el Perú de hoy* (Lima: ADEC-ATC, Asociación para el Desarrollo, 1992).

6. In conjunction with other events, the strikes increased pressure on the Morales Bermúdez government to leave power. The Velasco and Morales Bermúdez periods are discussed in Stephen M. Gorman, ed., *Post-Revolutionary Peru: The Politics of Transformation* (Boulder: Westview Press, 1982). The transition period is discussed in Nicolás Lynch, *La transición conservadora: Movimiento social y democracia en el Perú, 1975–78* (Lima: El zorro del abajo ediciones, 1992); Henry Pease García, *Los caminos del poder: Tres años de crisis en la escena política* (Lima: DESCO, Centro de Estudios y Promoción del Desarrollo, 1979). The elite dynamics of the transition to democracy are described in Catherine M. Conaghan and James M. Malloy, *Unsettling Statecraft: Democracy and Neoliberalism in the Central Andes* (Pittsburgh: University of Pittsburgh Press, 1994).

7. For a study of the development of university radicalism, see Nicolás Lynch, *Los jovenes rojos de San Marcos: El radicalismo universitario de los años setenta* (Lima: El zorro de abajo ediciones, 1990). For a study of the estrangement of young factory workers from the Left in the 1980s, see Fernando Rospigliosi, *Juventud obrera y partidos de izquierda: De la dictadura a la democracia* (Lima: Instituto de Estudios Peruanos, 1988).

8. For another study that identifies workers' aspirations for autonomy as a key factor influencing their political behavior and relationship to trade unionism, see the analysis of miners by Joshua DeWind, "Continuing to Be Peasants: Union

Militancy among Peruvian Miners," in *Workers' Control in Latin America, 1930–79,* ed. Jonathan C. Brown (Chapel Hill: University of North Carolina Press, 1997), 244–69.

9. For an analysis of the problems in the Left, see Kenneth Roberts, "Economic Crisis and the Demise of the Legal Left in Peru," *Comparative Politics* 29 (October 1996): 69–92; Maxwell A. Cameron, *Democracy and Authoritarianism in Peru: Political Coalitions and Social Change* (New York: St. Martin's Press, 1994), 77–96; Martín Tanaka, *Los espejismos de la democracia: El colapso del sistema de partidos en el Perú* (Lima: Instituto de Estudios Peruanos, 1998), 125–40.

10. To a certain degree, Parodi's book was overshadowed at the time by the appearance and marketing of another book published in the same year by Hernando de Soto, *El otro sendero* (Lima: Instituto Libertad y Democracia, 1986). De Soto's analysis also highlighted the centrality of the informal sector and its workers but used the analysis as a vehicle to launch an attack on "mercantilism" and the role of the state in Peru. De Soto's radical antistatism made him a hero of the Right, both in Peru and abroad. Mario Vargas Llosa, the Peruvian novelist who became the presidential candidate of the center-right in the 1990 election, was especially taken with De Soto's analysis. He wrote the preface to the English-language edition of the book published as *The Other Path: The Invisible Revolution in the Third World,* trans. June Abbott (New York: Harper & Row, 1989). Years later, however, Vargas Llosa and de Soto parted company after they exchanged personal insults in print and on Peruvian television.

11. For an overview of the problems of the García presidency, see John Crabtree, *Peru under García: An Opportunity Lost* (London: Macmillan, 1992); Carol Graham, *Peru's APRA: Parties, Politics and the Elusive Quest for Democracy* (Boulder: Lynne Rienner, 1992).

12. For an analysis of the heterodox economic policies of this period, see Ricardo Lago, "The Illusion of Pursuing Redistribution through Macropolicy: Peru's Heterodox Experience," in *The Macroeconomics of Populism in Latin America,* ed. Rudiger Dornbusch and Sebastian Edwards (Chicago: University of Chicago Press, 1991), 263–330; Eva Paus, "Adjustment and Development in Latin America: The Failure of Peruvian Heterodoxy, 1985–90," *World Development* 19 (1991): 411–34.

13. The pivotal works that explain the origins of Sendero are Gustavo Gorriti, *The Shining Path,* trans. Robin Kirk (Chapel Hill: University of North Carolina Press, 1999); and Carlos Iván Degregori, *El surgimento de Sendero Luminoso* (Lima: Instituto de Estudios Peruanos, 1990). Also see the collected essays in David Scott Palmer, ed., *The Shining Path of Peru* (New York: St. Martin's Press, 1992). For a discussion of Sendero's urban strategy in the 1990s, see Jo-Marie Burt, "Political Violence and the Grassroots in Lima, Peru," in *The New Politics of Inequality in Latin America: Rethinking Participation and Representation,* ed. Douglas Chalmers et al. (New York: Oxford University Press, 1997), 281–309. For an analysis of the decline of Sendero, see Carlos Iván Degregori et al., *Las rondas campesinas y la derrota de Sendero Luminoso* (Lima: Instituto de Estudios Peruanos, 1996); Carlos Tapia, *Las Fuerzas Armadas y Sendero Luminoso: Dos estrategias y un final* (Lima: Insti-

tuto de Estudios Peruanos, 1997). For the most recent synthesis of reflections on the origins and impact of Sendero, see Steve J. Stern, ed., *Shining and Other Paths: War and Society in Peru, 1980–1995* (Durham, N.C.: Duke University Press, 1998).

14. The 1990 campaign is analyzed in Carlos Iván Degregori and Romeo Grompone, *Elecciones 1990, demonios y redentores: Una tragedia en dos vueltas* (Lima: Instituto de Estudios Peruanos, 1991). Also see Cameron, *Democracy and Authoritarianism.* Mario Vargas Llosa wrote his memoirs of the campaign, *Pez en el agua* (Barcelona: Seix Barral, 1993). For a discussion of Fujimori's support among lower-class voters, see Aldo Panfichi, "The Authoritarian Alternative: 'Anti-Politics' in the Popular Sectors of Lima," in *The New Politics of Inequality in Latin America,* ed. Chalmers et al., 217–36.

15. For further analyses of the politics surrounding the auto-coup see Philip Mauceri, "State Reform, Coalitions, and the Neoliberal Autogolpe in Peru," *Latin American Research Review* 30 (1995): 7–37; Maxwell Cameron, "Self-Coups: Peru, Guatemala, and Russia," *Journal of Democracy* 9 (January 1998): 125–39; Catherine M. Conaghan, "Polls, Political Discourse and the Public Sphere: The Spin on Peru's Fuji-golpe," in *Latin America in Comparative Perspective: New Approaches to Methods and Analysis,* ed. Peter Smith (Boulder: Westview Press, 1995), 227–55.

16. To date, there are two important volumes on the Fujimori presidency: Maxwell A. Cameron and Philip Mauceri, eds., *The Peruvian Labyrinth: Polity, Society, Economy* (University Park: Pennsylvania State University Press, 1997); Fernando Tuesta, ed., *Los enigmas del poder, Fujimori, 1990–1996* (Lima: Fundación Friedrich Ebert, 1996). For a discussion of the populist dimensions of *Fujimorismo* see Kenneth M. Roberts, "Neoliberalism and the Transformation of Populism in Latin America: The Peruvian Case," *World Politics* 48 (1995): 82–116; Bruce H. Kay, "'Fujipopulism' and the Liberal State in Peru, 1990–95," *Journal of Inter-American Studies and World Affairs* 38 (Winter 1996): 55–98.

17. See his work in Luis Pásara and Jorge Parodi, eds., *Democracia, sociedad y gobierno en el Perú* (Lima: Centro de Estudios de Democracia y Sociedad, 1988); Jorge Parodi, ed., *Los pobres, la ciudad y la política* (Lima: Centro de Estudios de Democracia y Sociedad, 1993).

18. For analyses of a variety of Latin American social movements, see the essays in Sonia E. Alvarez, Evelina Dagnino, and Arturo Escobar, eds., *Cultures of Politics, Politics of Cultures: Re-Visioning Latin American Social Movements* (Boulder: Westview Press, 1998). Also see the essays in *The New Politics of Inequality in Latin America,* ed. Chalmers et al.

Introduction

1. Pedro Galín, "En torno a la clase obrera en el Perú," *Revista Apuntes* 15 (1985): 3–17.

2. Vanguardia Revolucionaria was one of several Maoist parties that were part of Peru's New Left. It was originally founded in 1965 and incorporated Trotskyites, former Communist Party members, a rebel faction of the Movimiento Iz-

quierda Revolucionario, and dissidents from Belaúnde's Acción Popular. VR formed an electoral coalition in 1980, Alianza Revolucionaria de Izquierda (ARI), with other radical parties, including Patria Roja and MIR.

Chapter 1

1. Departments are the subnational administrative units of the government. There are currently twenty-four departments in Peru. The departments are subdivided into provinces; provinces are broken down into districts.

Chapter 2

1. Jorge Parodi, "Las debilidades organizativas del gremio metalúrgico: Hablan los dirigentes," in *La Federación Metalúrgica: Historia y problemas* (Lima: CEDAL, 1982), 106.

2. In its initial organization, Metal Empresa organized the workforce into groups and the groups were assigned specific tasks on a daily basis. These groups were not highly specialized and performed a variety of tasks. The company designated a leader for each group. In 1970, the factory was organized into sections. Supervisors designated for each section assigned specific tasks to workers; thus the groups and group leaders were eliminated.

3. Camilo Torres was a Colombian priest who became a guerrilla insurgent. His work with the poor led him to political radicalism. He left the priesthood in 1965 to join the Ejército de Liberación Nacional (ELN). He was killed in his first military encounter with government troops in 1965.

4. Ernesto "Che" Guevara was an Argentine-born doctor who joined Fidel Castro and became a notable leader in the guerrilla insurgency that culminated in the Cuban Revolution of 1959. He went on to hold high-level positions in the revolutionary government. Guevara became an ardent advocate of spreading revolution across Latin America, and his ideas (*Guevarismo*) shaped an entire generation of the Latin American Left. He was killed in Bolivia in 1967 by government troops after leading a failed guerrilla insurgency.

Chapter 3

1. "Evaluación: La dirección política-sindical en la base de ME (Metal Empresa)," Internal document of the cell of the Partido Comunista Revolucionario "Trinchera Roja," 11 March 1980, photocopy.

2. Jorge Parodi, "Las debilidades organizativas del gremio metalúrgico: Hablan los dirigentes," in *La Federación Metalúrgica: Historia y problemas,* ed. Giovanni Bonfiglio and Jorge Parodi (Lima: CEDAL, 1982), 128.

3. For a description of the competition among parties to control unions and its effects on the organization of congresses and federations, see Carmen Rosa

Balbi and Jorge Parodi, "Los límites de la izquerda: El caso sindical," *La Revista* 5 (July 1981).

4. "Informe de la situación de la base," Internal document of the Metal Empresa cell of Vanguardia Revolucionaria, 29 March 1977, photocopy.

5. Ibid.

6. José Carlos Mariátegui was a leading journalist and intellectual in Peru in the 1920s. His most noted works were published in *Seven Interpretative Essays on Peruvian Reality* (Austin: University of Texas Press, 1971). In 1929, he helped found the Socialist Party, which later became an affiliate of the Communist International. He died in 1930 at the age of thirty-five. His ideas became pivotal in the debates in the Peruvian Left.

7. See the previously cited "Evaluación" of Trinchera Roja.

Chapter 4

1. Giovanni Bonfiglio, "Historia de la Federación Metalúrgica," in *La Federación Metalúrgica: Historia y problemas hoy* (Lima: CEDAL, 1983), 11–61.

2. Jorge Parodi, "Las debilidades organizativas del gremio metalúrgico: Hablan los dirigentes," in *La Federación Metalúrgica: Historia y problemas,* ed. Giovanni Bonfiglio and Jorge Parodi (Lima: CEDAL, 1982), 100.

3. Ibid., 125.

4. Ibid., 98.

5. Jorge Parodi, "La desmovilización del sindicalismo industrial peruano durante el segundo Belaundismo," Instituto de Estudios Peruanos, 1983, 1–29.

6. Parodi, "Las debilidades," 101.

7. Ibid.

8. Ibid., 106.

9. Ibid., 113–31.

Chapter 5

1. This group was identified on the basis of information provided by several workers in the plant and does not encompass the workforce of the plant in its entirety.

2. Personal communication with Dr. Alberto Seguín.

Chapter 6

1. Hugo Blanco began his political career as an organizer of the peasant union movement in the La Convención Valley in the southern province of Cuzco in 1958. After clashes between the peasant organizations and police, Blanco was arrested in 1966 and received a death sentence. His sentence was commuted by President Juan Velasco Alvarado and he was set free. In 1978, Blanco was elected to the constituent assembly on the ticket of the Frente Obrero Campesino, Estudiantil y

Popular (FOCEP), receiving the most votes of any candidate of the Left. In 1980, he was elected to the Chamber of Deputies of the congress.

Javier Diez Canseco joined Vanguardia Revolucionaria (VR) in 1967. As leader of VR, he was elected to serve in the constituent assembly as part of the left-wing coalition, Unidad Democrático Popular (UDP). In 1983, he was elected as secretary general of the Partido Unificado Mariateguista (PUM). He has served in every Peruvian legislature from 1980 to 2000, with the exception of the postcoup constituent assembly of 1993–95.

Chapter 13

1. Ricardo Letts was one of the co-founders of Vanguardia Revolucionaria in 1965. In 1970, he was head of the party's national political commission. He served as secretary general of the party from 1978 through 1972. He lost his seat in congress when President Fujimori shut down the legislature in the auto-coup of 5 April 1992. Letts subsequently retired from politics.

2. Edmundo Murrugarra was co-founder of Vanguardia Revolucionaria in 1965. In 1970, he headed the party's national political committee. He was elected to serve as a senator in the congress in 1980, 1985, and 1990. He lost his senate seat when President Fujimori shut down the congress in the auto-coup of 5 April 1992. He subsequently retired from politics.

Epilogue

1. Statistics compiled by the Ministerio de Industria, Turismo, Integración y Negociaciones Comerciales Internacionales. They were published in Richard Webb and Graciela Fernández Baca, *Perú en numeros 1993* (Lima: Cuánto, 1994), 445.

2. The index of employment in manufacturing registered the following figures: 1980 = 101.9, 1985 = 85.0, 1990 = 82.9, 1991 = 78.7, 1992 = 70.6. Figures are taken from Webb and Fernández, *Perú,* 275.

3. Ibid., 270.

4. Francisco Verdera, "El mercado de trabajo de Lima metropolitana: Estructura y evolución, 1970–1990," Working Paper, Instituto de Estudios Peruanos, March 1994, photocopy, 21.

5. Webb and Fernández, *Perú,* 289.

6. Underemployment is defined as a situation in which an individual works thirty-five or fewer hours per week and receives a wage below the legal minimum wage of January 1967 based on adjustments to the consumer price index. Acute underemployment means that income is below one-third of that used to measure underemployment. The definitions and statistics are taken from Ministerio de Trabajo y Promoción Social, *Anuario estadístico 1994* (Lima: Ministerio de Trabajo y Promoción Social, 1994). Figures are from Webb and Fernández, *Perú,* 270.

7. Data taken from author's count of the events as documented by DESCO in the weekly bulletin of *Resumen Semanal,* 1984.

8. Carmen Rosa Balbi, "La recesión silenciosa," *Quehacer* 59 (June–July 1989): 17.

9. Webb and Fernández, *Perú,* 276.

10. Jorge Parodi, "Los sindicatos en la democracia vacia," in *Democracia, sociedad y gobierno en el Perú* (Lima: Centro de Estudios de Democracia y Sociedad, 1988), 79–124.

11. Javier Neves, "Derechos laborales: Queja con cola," *Quehacer* 88 (March–April 1994): 46–50.

12. "La reforma laboral en debate," *Cuadernos Laborales* 100 (May 1994): 51.

13. Jorge Parodi, "Entre la Utopia y la tradición: Izquierda y democracia en los municipios de los pobladores," in *Los pobres, la ciudad y la política,* ed. Jorge Parodi (Lima: Centro de Estudios de Democracia y Sociedad), 145–55.

14. Werner Garate, *El sindicalismo a inicios de los anos noventa: Una aproximación cuantitativa* (Lima: ADEC, 1993): 20.

15. Fernando Rospigliosi, *Juventud obrera y partidos de Izquierda* (Lima: Instituto de Estudios Peruanos, 1988).

16. Garate, *El sindicalismo,* 53.

17. Verdera, "El mercado," 21.

18. Julio Franco, "Explosión de los servicios," *Cuadernos Laborales* 106 (November 1994): 24–26.

19. Carmen Rosa Balbi, "Senderos Minados," *Quehacer* (October–November 1989): 57.

20. Carmen Rosa Balbi, "Sendero y los sindicatos," *Debate* 65 (August–September 1991): 18.

21. Rospigliosi, *Juventud.*

22. Jorge Parodi and Walter Twanama, "Los pobres, la ciudad y la política: Un estudio de actitudes," in *Los pobres,* ed. Parodi, 66–89.

23. Gonzalo Portocarrero and Rafael Tapia, *Trabajadores, sindicalismo y política en el Perú de hoy* (Lima: Asociación Laboral para el Desarrollo ADEC-ATC, 1993), 46.

24. Ibid., 113.

25. Ibid., 40.

Index

Acción Popular, 32, 126, 130

AFL-CIO, 155

Aguilar, Pedro, 86–87

Alianza Popular Revolucionaria Americana (APRA): demonstrations, 68; employer collaboration, 31; oligarchy ties, 32; Unión Grauina, 125; work stoppage against, 60

Alianza Revolucionaria de la Izquierda (ARI), 124

Allende, Salvador, 58

APRA. *See* Alianza Popular Revolucionaria Americana

Apurímac, 129, 148, 149

Argolla system: avoiding, 34; clientelism, xii; large industries, 30; limits, 136; pro-union movement, 34–35; talareños in, 25–26; threat of exclusion, 137; unionization, 36; as worker control, 25–26, 136; Zúñiga's view of, 107

ARI. *See* Alianza Revolucionaria de la Izquierda

Barreda, César, 123

Belaúnde Terry, Fernando: Metal Empresa collaboration, 105–6; noncompliance with union agreements, 93; timid reformism, 32

Benefits: clasista strategy, 39, 139; company losses claimed, 113; equality of, 137; unionization, 36; worker perspective, 54; Zúñiga's view of, 109–11

Berríos, Telósofo, 129

Birth control, 121

Blanco, Hugo, 95, 168–69 (n. 1)

Boilermakers, 49

Callao, 145

Caller, Laura, 121

Cambio 90–Nueva Mayoría movement, xvii, xviii–xix

Caritas del Perú, 146

Catholic Church, 32

Caudillismo, 57, 69, 140

Cerro de Pasco mine, 59

CGTP. *See* Confederación General de Trabajadores del Perú

Children: future of, 92; labor of, 99–101; malnutrition, 90, 91

Chile: marches supporting, 58, 59, 64; privatization in, 148

Chincheros, 130

Civil liberties, 64

Clase Obrera, 123

Clasismo, xiii, xix; benefits vs. ideology, 62; defined, 4

Clasista trade unionism: class struggle and la lucha, xiii–xiv, 38, 139–40, 141–42; demand making, 41–42; disillusionment, 54–55; divisions, 123; economic realities of 1980s, 142; estrangement from workers, 46; everyday politics and, 70–71; incentives policy, 49–51; intermediary role of leader, 47; leadership image and, 66; leadership union, 55; Left fragmentation, 52; leftist groups, 61; limits of, 140–42; meaning, in practice, 61; pact broken, 55; passive, 96; question of principles, 46; radicalism, 138; sacrifices of leaders, 53; structure and party ties, 62; weaknesses, 70, 123; worker identity, 140

Clientelism: Fujimori, xix; leftist groups, 47

Cobriza, 59

Collective consciousness: conflict with company interests, 28; emergence, 30; leaders' view of, 55; oppression and, 27–28; organizing the poor, 117; party training, 62; passive, 96; serranos, 118; unionization, 30

Communist Party: argolla system, 31;

firing of union leaders, 117; military government, 65; revisionists, 65; Velasco support, xiv; youth/student movement, 33

Confederación Campesina del Perú, 130

Confederación General de Trabajadores del Perú (CGTP): firing of union leaders, 123; mobilizing workers, 51; party and unions, 63; Velasco support, xiv; work stoppage, 60

Consejo Nacional de Ciencia y Tecnología (CONCYTEC; National Council of Science and Technology), 147

Construction industry, 10; frequent layoffs, 14; self-employment and, 81; Zúñiga in, 11–12

Consumption vs. saving, 76, 81, 82–84

Contracts, labor, 25

Cooperación Popular, 126–27, 131

Corporación del Desarrollo de Apurímac, 127, 128–29

Cotler, Julio, 8

Criollos: consumption vs. saving, 83–84; interviewed, 6; manual labor, 22; personal connections, 17; vs. serranos, 17, 19–20, 37, 136; social mobility expectations, 21; weekend work, 82; work ethic, 18, 20, 81, 108

Cronyism, 136. See also Argolla system; Clientelism

Cuba, 114, 115

Cuban Revolution, 33, 167 (n. 4)

Curpahuasi district, 125, 126, 127

Cuzco, 99–100

Demonstrations, attendance at, 67–69, 140

De Soto, Hernando, 165 (n. 10)

Diez Canseco, Javier, 95, 124, 169 (n. 1, chap. 12)

District Social Center of Curpahuasi and Anexos, 125, 147

Downsizing: clasista analysis, 50; severance packages, 49–50, 77

Economic crisis of 1980s: effect on unions, 142, 143; effects on workers, xii; worker militancy, xv, 153

Economy: deterioration in 1970s, 69; export, 135; Fuji-shock, 146–47, 148, 153–54; García phase, xvii, 144, 151; real wages in 1980s and 1990s, 152

Education: for children, 92, 144; construction work, 14–15; limeño advantages, 16–17, 21–22; Metal Empresa requirements, 23; migrants, 136; peasants, 129; in provinces, 99, 100; requirements for skilled factory workers, 11; technical, 17; union courses, 116; union leaders, 44; university in Apurímac, 129; Zúñiga's, 99, 100, 102; of Zúñiga's children, 144–45

Equality among workers, 28, 30; skilled workers, 48; in treatment, 47; and unionization, 36, 37, 137

Fábrica Nacional de Licores Poblete, 146

Family leave benefit, 109–10; before unionization, 24–25; as politically significant, 117

Federación de Pescadores, 34

Federación de Trabajadores de la Industria Metalúrgica del Perú (FETIMP): as central command, 57; clasismo as dictatorial, 69; clasista influence, 61; decline, 69; factionalism, 67; membership, 57; Metal Empresa union leadership, 6; mutual support, 57–61; negotiations for governing council, 66–67; participation in collective action, 69; solidarity, 58, 64; strikes, 60

FETIMP. See Federación de Trabajadores de la Industria Metalúrgica del Perú

Fishermen's unions, 34, 58, 59

Foco model, 38

Foreign debt, 148

Free trade, 148

Frente Obrero Campesino, Estudiantil y Popular (FOCEP), 168–69 (n. 1)

Fujimori, Alberto: electoral strategy, xvii–xviii; fujimorismo as political project, xviii–xix; political agenda, 154–55; self-coup (auto-golpe), xviii, 148; technocratic antipolitics, xii; weakening unions, 153–54

Fuji-shock: conditions after, 146–47, 148; malnutrition, 146; Sendero Luminoso, 156–57

Gallardo, Angel, 3

García, Alan: economic crisis and terrorism, 151; economic policies, xvii, 144, 151; honeymoon phase, xvi–xvii; labor laws liberalized, 155; populist policies, 153

General Strike of 1976, 49, 51–52, 60

Government: as institutional actor, 40–41; militant collective action, 61; noninterference principle, 58

Guevara, Ernesto "Che," 32, 38, 167 (n. 4)

Hours and wages, 25

Household economy, 87–90, 142, 138

Housing, 145

Huayno music, 125

Hunger strikes, 153

Hyperinflation, xvii, xviii

ILO. *See* International Labor Organization

Incentives policy, 46, 75, 76; clasista analysis, 49–50

Industrial Community Law, xii, 39

Industrial sector, growth and crisis in, 135, 151–52, 169 (n. 2)

Industrial workers. *See* Workers

Inflation, xvii

Informal sector: de Soto analysis, 165 (n. 10); economic change, 135; economic crisis and, 152; worker security/status vs., 91

Informants, company, 25–26

International Labor Organization (ILO), 154, 155

Interunion activity: caudillos and overall strength, 69; clasista leadership, 140; Left, 63; solidarity, 57, 95

Izquierda Unida, xv, 129; elections of 1995, xviii; neglect of workers, 132; split, xvii

Job classification systems, 45–46

Job security: approval of military government, 65; distrust of company, 93–94; as early achievement, 135–36; economic independence vs., 3–4; Law of Security of Employment, 16; on-the-job accidents staged, xiii, 16; police clearances, 14; Promecán example, 72–73; unionization and, 35; union paternalism, 43

Labor laws, xii; Fujimori, 155; neoliberalism, xix

Labor surplus, 18–19, 25, 39

Law of Employer Entitlement (1993), 154

Law of Security of Employment, xii–xiii; probationary period, 16; unionization, 35; workers' enthusiasm for, 16

Leaders/leadership: abilities analyzed, 54; collective action, 65; communicative role, 44; competition, 52–53; consulting other unions, 58; defending the absent, 132; defense of individual workers, 44–45; family woes, 122; firing after general strike, 94, 117; first strike, 112–13; ideological disputes, 52–53; interviews, 6, 7; isolation of militants, xv–xvi; leader-follower relationship, 42–44; leave time for, 110; leftist parties relationship, 71; loyalty or trust, 66; march and demonstration attendance, 68; mistrust of, 56; origins, 42–43; pact with workers, 43; party influence, 63–64; personal costs, 56; police repression, 67; political influences, 6; potential, 30–31; power and moral authority, 42; Promecán closure, 105; quitting factory work, 53–54; rank and file dissent, 46; resentment of, 54–55; respect for, 66–67; sacrifices, 53, 116; severance pay, 124; small business prospects, 5; as social polyglot, 44; strained relationship with rank and file, xv, 50, 52; trade-off with workers, 55; trust of workers, 46; violent tactics, 96–97; worker dependency, 43–44; work stoppage (1981), 94; Zúñiga's view of, 114–15

Leave time for union activity, 110

Left: achievements, xiv; critique of, 71; election of 1990, xviii; electoral aspirations, xv; fragmentation and disarray, 52; ideological training, 61–62; interunion activity, 63; leadership of la lucha, 139; New Left, 32, 38; production costs, 124; wage depreciation, 117; worker identities, xiv

Letts, Ricardo, 115, 169 (n. 1, chap. 13)

Liberation theology, 32

Lima, 135

Limeños: educational advantages, 16–17;

personal connections, 17; as shirkers, 108

Lockouts, employer, 137, 154

Lucha, la: benefits strategy, 39; clasismo, xiii–xiv, 140–41; concept of, 38; conditions for strike, 38–39; in diverse urban environments, 138; fired union leaders, 123; metallurgical unions' commitment, 47, 140; as modus operandi, 41; necessity of, 138

Luna Vargas, Andrés, 115, 123, 126

Maestranza section, 48

Malnutrition, xvi, 90, 91, 146

Management: authority after unionization, 45; criollo/serrano differences, 37; negotiating approach, 39; noncompliance with agreements, 93; treatment before unionization, 107

Manual labor: criollo attitudes, 22; metal manufacturing, 23

Manufacturing: employment index, 169 (n. 2, epilogue); importance in economy, 5; recent production figures, 151–52

Marches, 51, 54; attendance at, 67–69; police repression, 67; supporting Chile, 58, 59, 64

Mariátegui, José Carlos, 52, 168 (n. 6, chap. 3)

Marxism, xi; liberation theology, 32; party members, 62–63

Mechanics, 15

Metal Empresa: clasista leadership reassessed, 56; commercial logic of, 136; description, 5; discipline, 24; education requirements, 23; financial records, 39–40, 41, 113; founding, 23; government collaboration, 105–6; migrants vs. city-born workers, 11; negotiations, 138; noncompliance with agreements, 92–93, 143; as representative, 5; shift work, 23–24; worker distrust, 92, 93–94; workers leaving, 77–79; working conditions, 107; work organization, 167 (n. 2, chap. 2)

Metallurgical industry: labor skills, 23; profits and wages, 28–29, 113; recent production statistics, 152; technological

innovation, 47–48; unionization, 31; work routine, 105

Metallurgical unions. *See* Federación de Trabajadores de la Industria Metalúrgica del Perú

Middle class, urban, 31–34

Military government: approval of, 65; authoritarianism, 50–51, 64; collective displays of force against, 64–65; company perspective, 93; fate of clasismo, 70; Left opposition, 139; nature of, xi; radicalism by unions, 64; struggle against, 65; student opposition, 33; support declining, 65; worker mobilization, 50–51

Mineworkers' unions, 58, 59

Mining, 99, 100, 101, 115, 147

Ministry of Labor, 40–41, 112

Moonlighting, 85

Morales Bermúdez, Francisco, 94, 117, 123

Motor Perú, 60

Murrugarra, Edmundo, 115–16, 169 (n. 2, chap. 13)

New Left groups, 32, 38

Newspaper, union, 44, 53, 92

Oblitas, Américo, 128

Overtime pay: family expenses, 72; Zúñiga's opportunities for, 73–75

Pacheco, Feliciano, 54

Paper industry, 4

Parodi, Jorge, xi; complaint against, 7; original publication of book, xvi–xvii; later activities, xix

Part-time workers, 155

Pastor, Néstor, 123

Paternalism, 29–30; unions, 43, 140

Peasants, 82, 128, 129

Penalty system, 24

Plásticos El Pacífico, 60

Poblete Vidal, Jacinto, 146

Political education, 61–62

Political parties, 148, 154–55

Politics: diverging views of, 70–71; Zúñiga's view of, 116–17

"Popular" sectors. See *Sectores populares*

Populist model, 153

Portilla, Hernán, 129

Portocarrero, Gonzalo, 157

Profits: company's financial records, 40, 41, 113; job insecurity, 73; technological innovation, 47; wages and, 28–29, 30

Profit sharing, xii–xiii

Promecán: bankruptcy, 23; closure as political move, 105–6; worker fears, 35, 73; Zúñiga's experience, 104–6

Purchasing power, xvi, 72, 82; inflation and, 85

Quintanilla, Lino, 115

Quiroz, Delmer, 42–43, 54, 114

Radicalism, 64–65; belligerence, 142; clasista unionism and, 138; emphasis criticized, 70

Retirement packages. *See* Severance packages

Revisionists, 65

Salazar, Julio "Chino," 73–74, 114, 119–20

Saving vs. consumption, 76, 81, 82–84

Sea, Gilberto, 126

Secretaría de Asistencia Social (Secretariat of Social Welfare), 45, 111

Sectores populares: aspirations of, 10; term, 139

Self-employment: capitalist mentality, 3; and cutbacks at factory, 4; future prospects, 157; home ownership and, 76; job security, 73; and plant closures, 91–92; serrano migrants, 79–82; and severance pay, 77, Zúñiga's, 73–74, 119–20

Self-improvement, drive for, 79–80, 84

Sendero Luminoso, xvii; reasons for, 41; worker support for, 156–57

Serrano migration: economic diversification, 76–77; high expectations, 10; mentality and progress, 79–80, 142; nature of migrant life, xi; networks of relatives and friends, 11–13; new outlook, 124; relative identities, 135; self-employment, 79–82; stresses, 82; unionization and, 137; worker status, 136

Serranos: vs. criollos, 17, 19–20, 37, 136; as epithet, 19–20; good relations with

bosses, 26–27; interviewed, 6; machinists, 19; obedience, 17–19; talareño pressure on, 26; as true Peruvians, 118; work ethic, 17, 19, 20, 107–8. See also *Serrano* migration

Severance packages: clasista analysis, 50; economic recession conditions, xv; job security issue, 77; as opportunities, 142; and self-employment, 4; union leaders, 124; Zúñiga's experience, 120

Sheet metal industry. *See* Metallurgical industry

Sider-Perú, 59

Sindicato de Construcción Civil de Callao, 34

Skill acquisition by serranos: collective consciousness, 29; future prospects, 136; Zúñiga's experience, 104

Skilled workers: advantages for migrants, 10; technological innovation, 47–49; union leadership, 55

Social assistance loans, 24–25, 36, 45

Social class analysis, 62

Socialist Party, 168 (n. 6, chap. 3)

Social mobility, xiv, 10; serranos, 21, 22

Social security contributions, 92

Solidarity: among unions, 57; radicalism and, 65; workers' view, 64, 109; work stoppages, 51–52

Squatters, 118

Standard of living: decline in 1980s, 87–90; factory wages, 76–77

Stress, 82; and job security, 90–91

Strike(s): of 19 July 1977, 123; conditions for, 38–39; Federación Metalúrgica and, 55; first, 112–13; hunger, 153; instances of, 59–60; solidarity disintegrating, 95; strikebreakers and, 156; temporary workers and, 156; youth movement, 34

Strike threats, 35; as clasista strategy, 39; necessity of, 41; and productivity issues, 47; among unions, 57–61; as weapon, 138

Students: police repression, 67; political party, 114; radicalization, 32–33; as urban middle class, 31–34; and workers, xiv, 62–63, 139

Supplementary income strategies, 85–87, 142–43

INDEX

Talareños: argolla system, 25–26; ties with bosses, 13; types, in clasista analysis, 36–37; Zúñiga's view of, 107

Teachers' union, 123

Technocrats, xii

Temporary workers, 155–56

Terrorism, 156–57

Torres, Camilo, 33, 167 (n. 3)

Trinchera Roja, 53, 123

UDP. _See_ Unidad Democrática Popular

Unemployment, 92, 152

Unidad Democrática Popular (UDP), 124

Union, at Metal Empresa, 5–6; accomplishments summarized, 137–38; courses, 116; destruction threatened, 93–94; expansion under Velasco, xiii; negotiations questioned, 39; pragmatism of workers, xv; preventive measures against, 25; relationships, kinds of, 47; threatening language, 94

Unión Grauina, 126–31, 147

Unionization: authority of management, 45; collective consciousness, 30; obstacles, 31; petition drive, 35; process, 30–31; prounion movement, 34–35; university students, 34

Union life, 137–38

Union negotiations, restrictions on, 64

Unions: attendance at rallies/marches, 67–68; Belaúnde era, 153; caudillos, 69; Fujimori regulations, 153–54, 155–56; leave time for activity related to, 110; leftist parties, 154; recent unemployment, 152–53; and Sendero Luminoso, 156–57; worker-management relations, 27

Unitario de Lucha, 58

Universidad Nacional de Agraria, 34

Universidad Nacional de Ingeniería, 34

Universities, 33, 34, 38

Urban settlers, 138–39

Vanguardia Revolucionaria (VR): divisions, 123; ideological disputes, 53; leaders, 169 (nn. 1, 2, chap. 13); Metal Empresa linkage, 5; organizing drive, 33–34; origins, 166–67 (n. 2); party cell, 62–63; political training, 61–62; sacrifices of union leaders, 116; students, 114; student-worker relationship, 62–63; Unión Grauina, 126

Vargas Llosa, Mario, xviii, 165 (n. 10)

Velasco Alvarado, Juan: action-oriented unionism, 61; demonization, xii; nature of military government, xi; rally, 121; union expansion, xiii

Violence: political, 156; reactive behavior, 94–96; rhetoric of, 94; selective execution, 157

VR. _See_ Vanguardia Revolucionaria

Wages: in 1980s and 1990s, 152; after unionization, 72; before union, 24–27; ceilings on, 153; construction vs. sheet metal industry, 104; depreciation, 117; inflation, 85; profits and, 28–29, 30; raises, 25; unionization, 36

Welders, 48–49

White-collar employment, 22

Work, attitudes toward: of serranos vs. criollos, 17, 18, 81; Zúñiga's, 107–8

Workers: benefits emphasis, 55; defense of individual, 43; dependent attitudes, 43–44; dissatisfaction under Fujimori, 156; distrust of company, 92, 93–94; early achievements, 135–36; later conditions, 151; marches and police repression, 67; mobilization potential, 42; passivity, 96; political unionism, xv; as privileged, 5; as producers of wealth, 137; resentment of union leaders, 54–55; solidarity, 65–66; struggle, xi; youth of, 65

Working class, as revolutionary agent, xvi, 5, 27

Working conditions: company perspective, 24; improvements vis-à-vis larger changes, 55; and stress, 90–91; and unionization, 35–37

Work stoppages: clasista analysis, 51; decline, 69; expelled workers, 94; instances of, 59–60; solidarity, 51–52. _See also_ Strike(s)

Youth movement, 43

Zúñiga Sotomayor, Jesús: background in provinces, 99–101; chicken ranch venture, 73–74; early life in Lima, 102–3; factory experience, 104–6; lack of overtime pay, 73; later experiences, xix, 144–49; marriage and children, 121–22; as migrant, xi; oral history discussed, 8; quits factory, 54; retirement, 123–24

Zúñiga Vargas, Wenceslao, 99–100, 102